PERFECT IN WEAKNESS

Reel Spirituality Monograph Series

SERIES DESCRIPTION

The Reel Spirituality Monograph Series features a collection of theoretically precise yet readable essays on a diverse set of film-related topics, each of which makes a substantive contribution to the academic exploration of Theology and Film. The series consists of two kinds of works: 1) popular-level introductions to key concepts in and practical applications of the Theology and Film discipline, and 2) methodologically rigorous investigations of theologically significant films, filmmakers, film genres, and topics in cinema studies. The first kind of monograph seeks to introduce the world of Theology and Film to a wider audience. The second seeks to expand the academic resources available to scholars and students of Theology and Film. In both cases, these essays explore the various ways in which "the cinema" (broadly understood to include the variety of audio-visual storytelling forms that continues to evolve along with emerging digital technologies) contributes to the overall shape and trajectory of the contemporary cultural imagination. The larger aim of producing both scholarly and popular-level monographs is to generate a number of resources for enthusiasts, undergraduate and graduate students, and scholars. As such, the Reel Spirituality Monograph Series ultimately exists to encourage the enthusiast to become a more thoughtful student of the cinema and the scholar to become a more passionate viewer.

PERFECT IN WEAKNESS
Faith in Tarkovsky's Stalker

COLIN HEBER-PERCY

CASCADE *Books* • Eugene, Oregon

PERFECT IN WEAKNESS
Faith in Tarkovsky's *Stalker*

Reel Spirituality Monograph Series

Copyright © 2019 Colin Heber-Percy. All rights reserved. Except for brief quotations in critical publications or reviews, no part of this book may be reproduced in any manner without prior written permission from the publisher. Write: Permissions, Wipf and Stock Publishers, 199 W. 8th Ave., Suite 3, Eugene, OR 97401.

Cascade Books
An Imprint of Wipf and Stock Publishers
199 W. 8th Ave., Suite 3
Eugene, OR 97401

www.wipfandstock.com

PAPERBACK ISBN: 978-1-5326-6324-6
HARDCOVER ISBN: 978-1-5326-6325-3
EBOOK ISBN: 978-1-5326-6326-0

Cataloguing-in-Publication data:

Names: Heber-Percy, Colin.

Title: Perfect in weakness : faith in Tarkovsky's *Stalker* / by Colin Heber-Percy.

Description: Eugene, OR: Cascade Books, 2019 | Reel Spirituality Monograph Series | Includes bibliographical references.

Identifiers: ISBN 978-1-5326-6324-6 (paperback) | ISBN 978-1-5326-6325-3 (hardcover) | ISBN 978-1-5326-6326-0 (ebook)

Subjects: LCSH: Tarkovskiĭ, Andreĭ Arsen'evich, 1932–1986—Criticism and interpretation. | Science fiction—Religious aspects. | Motion pictures—Religious aspects.

Classification: PN1998.3.T36 H3 2019 (print) | PN1998.3.T36 (ebook)

All Scripture quotations are from the Holy Bible, New Revised Standard Version, Anglicized Edition, copyright © 1989, 1995. All rights reserved. Division of Christian Education of the National Council of the Churches of Christ in the United States of America.

Quotation from THE UNKNOWN UNIVERSITY by Roberto Bolaño. Copyright © 2013, Roberto Bolaño, used by permission of The Wylie Agency (UK) Ltd.

Manufactured in the U.S.A.   04/09/19

For Joseph, Theodore, and Agatha

cameram vobiscum intravi

Be one, be weak, keep moving

—Roberto Bolaño

CONTENTS

Acknowledgments | ix
Abbreviations | x

Introduction: Science Fiction and Faith | 1

1 Cracked Cisterns | 16

2 Journey | 27
    Journey   34
    Brocéliande   36
    La Mancha   41
    Sinai   43

3 The Kingdom of God | 54
    Apocalypse as Disaster   61
    Apocalypse as Revelation, and as Joke   64
    Apocalypse as Prophecy   69
    Apocalypse as Cinema   74
    Cinema as Icon   78

4 Faith | 84
5 Miracle | 100
   Coda | 110

   Bibliography | 113

ACKNOWLEDGMENTS

I would like to thank Dr Kutter Callaway and Elijah Davidson at The Fuller Theological Seminary for their invaluable support, guidance, and wisdom throughout.

I am grateful to Dr Robert Ellis at the University of Oxford for his initial encouragement to publish my work on *Stalker*.

But most of all, I would like to say the deepest, heartfelt thank you to my wife, Emma, for her love and patience while I journeyed into the Zone.

ABBREVIATIONS

AS *Acta Sanctorum Quotquot Toto Orbe Coluntur.* Edited by J. Bollandus and G. Henschenius. 68 vols. Antwerp and Brussels, 1643–1940.

PG *Patrologiae Cursus Completus: Series Graeca.* Edited by Jacques-Paul Migne. 162 vols. Paris, 1857–86.

PL *Patrologiae Cursus Completus: Series Latina.* Edited by Jacques-Paul Migne. 217 vols. Paris, 1844–64.

INTRODUCTION

Science Fiction and Faith

In the summer of 1972, David Bowie's "Starman" was a hit on both sides of the Atlantic. The song features an alien who waits in the sky and chooses to communicate his hopeful message through the radio. It is a message for a specific and selected subgroup within society, young people. The first-person narrator of the song hears the message, and excitedly phones a friend to see if they have heard it too. The phone call ends with a warning not to tell anyone about what they have heard; they might be locked up. The recipients of the saving message will not be believed; rather, they will be deemed mad.[1] The message these children have received must become for them at once a shared

---

1. Susan Sontag analyzes the elements of what she terms "a typical science-fiction plot." These stories always open, she says, with "the arrival of the thing. This is usually witnessed or suspected by one person, a young scientist on a field trip. Nobody, neither his neighbors nor his colleagues, will believe him for some time" (Sontag, "Imagination of Disaster," 209).

distinguishing marker, dangerous, even incriminating, and an article of faith. Here, neatly articulated by Bowie in a few lines, is the deep connection between Sontag's "typical science-fiction plot," and faith: the message, the community of the message, and the faith in that message that binds the community together and defines it.

> And their eyes were opened. Then Jesus sternly ordered them, "See that no one knows of this."[2]

At the center of these narratives is a dialectic of secrecy and prophecy, and it always plays out in the context of faith.

The same year Bowie released "Starman," J. Allen Hynek published *The UFO Experience: A Scientific Enquiry*, in which he broadly codified types of "alien encounter" testimony into six categories.[3] The categories are arranged in an ascending scale, from sightings of lights in the sky—like the lights the young people see through their window in Bowie's song—to close encounters—meetings with extraterrestrial life forms. In an effort to ground his analysis in a scientific methodology, Hynek endeavours to distinguish his data from elements that appear borrowed from science fiction, or which are, to his mind, straightforwardly cranky.

> The contactee cases are characterized by a "favored" human intermediary, an almost always solitary "contact man" who somehow has the special attribute of being able to see the UFOs and to communicate with their crew . . . The messages are usually addressed to all of humanity to "be good, stop fighting, live in love and brotherhood, ban the bomb, stop polluting the atmosphere" and other worthy platitudes. The

---

2. Matt 9:30 (NRSV).
3. Hynek, *UFO Experience*, 46–49.

Introduction

contactee often regards himself as messianically charged to deliver the message.[4]

In fact, of course, even as he dismisses as "pseudo-religious fanatics" with "low credibility values" those who claim to have been contacted in this way, Hynek falls neatly—if inadvertently—into the traditional sci-fi plot as recognized by Bowie and Sontag. The unbeliever is a crucial component in the story.

Five years after the publication of *The UFO Experience*, Steven Spielberg used Hynek's typology as the basis for and title of his hugely successful *Close Encounters of the Third Kind* (1977).

I am not going to discuss *Close Encounters* in any depth here; I turn to it simply because it serves as a well-known and well-loved introduction to a subgenre of science fiction cinema: the alien encounter movie. In order for a particular film to qualify as belonging to the alien encounter genre, I am going to insist, as I stated above, that films in this subgenre always address themselves to the psychological, philosophical, spiritual, or theological implications of that encounter.

Of course, there are many movies about aliens visiting earth that predate *Close Encounters*, but where Spielberg's movie is innovative (and normative for the subgenre I have tentatively identified) is in its overt recognition that alien encounter movies are not really about encounters with aliens at all. They are ways in which we encounter ourselves. Of course, as it stands, this is a cliché. But here I want to augment the cliché with Bowie's suggestion in "Starman" that these stories are very often (perhaps always) about encountering ourselves *in and through faith*. The characters in the narrative, and often we in the audience, are asked to

4. Hynek, *UFO Experience*, 47.

believe a message, a story, the reality of an encounter that will radically alter our understanding of the world or throw us up against a contrary prevailing view. It might free us; it might get us locked up.

So, all the films in this subgenre are concerned with faith in one form or another: as a last resort, as a survival mechanism, as a separating sign, as a call for countercultural solidarity, or as a harrowing absence. I am not going to offer an exhaustive list here, but as examples we could pick out for special mention Nicolas Roeg's *The Man Who Fell to Earth* (1976), which is ultimately about faith as mission, about trying (and failing) to keep faith with a loving goal in a faithless and loveless society; *K-Pax* (2001) is about faith as the fruit of trauma; or Philip Kaufman's extraordinary remake of *Invasion of the Bodysnatchers* (1978) in which faith in our fellow human beings becomes an exploitable vulnerability, rendering us open to attack from a parasitic alien vector. To have faith in no one, the film suggests, is ultimately the only hope of survival; it is also, of course, to know no one, to be alone.

In *Close Encounters* itself, the normalcy of the lives of Roy and Ronnie Neary (played by Richard Dreyfuss and Terri Garr), the immediately recognizable mundanities of their family life form the backdrop to a sympathetically and painfully observed depiction of faith as conversion.[5] In a particularly poignant scene Roy looks out the window at the weekend world going by: neighbors playing baseball, mowing lawns, washing cars. But inside, inside his house,

5. Roy Neary falls into a different category of Hynekian contactee: "These reporters are in no way 'special'. They are not religious fanatics; they are more apt to be policemen, businessmen, schoolteachers, and other respectable citizens" (Hynek, *UFO Experience*, 48). It is salutary to see how Hynek's crudity and crassness can be translated by talents like Spielberg and Dreyfuss into something subtle and moving. It takes genius to make a silk purse out of a sow's ear.

Introduction

inside his disintegrating marriage, inside his head, everything has changed for Roy. A conversion has taken place, symbolized in the scene by Roy being placed behind this partially reflective window: a perpetual cross-fade.

And yet Spielberg chooses to place us, the audience, in a privileged position, on the other side of the window, looking in. We know Roy is not delusional. We have authorial surety that Roy's faith in what he witnessed is not misplaced or mistaken. We experienced the encounter with him. We can understand his wife Ronnie's bafflement, her suspicions, her increasing exasperation. Questioned by her children about their father's beliefs in the extraterrestrials, she insists, "No, they're not for real."[6] But while we can understand her confusion and misgivings, we can share in none of them. Our own faith in the aliens is as solid and settled as Roy's, though we are not called to convince anyone else. Our neighbors in the seats around us are not mowing their lawns; they are not oblivious to the presence of the aliens as Roy's are. And it is precisely this that ought to alert us to our own ambiguous and unsettling position here. Just as Roy has been singled out for the starman's message, so have we. Along with Roy and the others on the bend in the road that night, we have been chosen. We know Ronnie is wrong to doubt him. And here *Close Encounters* lets us off the hook. Though we have witnessed the arrival of the aliens, we fall outside of Sontag and Bowie's sci-fi schema: we are not called to keep the faith, to proselytize, or to protect ourselves and our message from the unbeliever. So, while we might identify *with* the faithful, we cannot identify *as* the faithful.

So precisely who are the extraterrestrials here? We are somehow both outside (*extra*) the story—as aliens, as Spielberg—but inside as well, as Roy, alone in a faithless

6. Spielberg, *Close Encounters*.

and unbelieving world; we are visitors and visited, watchers and watched. This paradoxical, privileged place is no place, or no fixed place; by sitting still we are transported, vouchsafed a view back at ourselves. The screen becomes—at least partially—a mirror.

After all, a movie theater is a place of watching. That is what "theater" means, deriving as it does from the Greek word to watch, to behold, to observe—*theasthai*. It is sometimes suggested that an analogue of the same word lies at the root of "theology."[7] For the ancient Greeks, the gods are, above all, guards watching over us. The theater is a place where we can, briefly, become gods, watchers, visitors, aliens to ourselves, transcendent. So, for Hesiod, the gods are described as follows:

> Thrice countless are they on the rich-pastured earth, Zeus' immortal watchers [φύλακες] of mortal human beings, who watch over judgements and wickedness, clothed in darkness [ἠέρα].[8]

In the theater, clothed in darkness, we sit somehow between projector and screen, subjects but also objects of our own subjective gaze, watchers of humanity. Cinema is, therefore, arguably a particularly germane context in which to do *theo*logy. I want to probe the theology of two films in detail. Both films are outstanding examples of the alien encounter genre that expose the peculiarity of our place as watchers and watched in cinema. I want to explore in

---

7. See Heidegger, *Parmenides*, 104: "That which looks into all that is ordinary, the uncanny as showing itself in advance, is the originally looking one in the eminent sense: τὸ θεᾶον, i.e., τὸ θεῖον." Just as in English the word "divine" connotes the heavenly, the numinous, so "to divine" means to search out, to investigate, to discover. Plato offers an alternative etymology for *theos*. See *Crat*. 397d.

8. Hesiod, *Op*. 252–53.

Introduction

particular and in depth what these films have to say about the nature and role of faith. Both films deal with "visitors" or aliens in oblique and fascinating ways. One is a lauded classic, the other a largely overlooked contemporary masterpiece. So, in this first volume, we will look at Andrei Tarkovsky's *Stalker* (1979). And in the second, we shall turn to Jonathan Glazer's *Under the Skin* (2013). Each volume is intended to stand alone as a monograph, but I hope that, by pairing them, I am able to bring both films into some sort of dialogue. A little playfully perhaps, we could think of *Stalker* as our camera; after all, it is about a search for a mythical room or chamber, literally a *camera*. *Under the Skin* might therefore stand for our screen, concerned as it is with fakery, allure, masks, and surfaces, the blank onto which our fears and desires are projected. Paired, the films offer us cinema in microcosm. And I believe both are fundamentally concerned with the role faith plays in making us human. In *Stalker*, faith is folly and weakness, but at the same time it is the unsurrenderable ground of all human, fallible experience; in *Under the Skin*, faith is nothing less than the flesh, human nature itself. While *Stalker* is manifestly about belief, *Under the Skin*, like *Close Encounters*, hinges on a conversion experience. What is remarkable about *Under the Skin* is that the conversion is experienced by the alien. To be converted to faith, the film suggests, is to become human. And *vice versa*.

The concepts of conversion to faith and subjective experience form the central focus of Stephen B. Bevans's transcendental model of contextual theology, according to which

> There are some things that we cannot understand without a complete change of mind. Some

things demand a radical shift in perspective, a
change in horizon—a *conversion*—before they
begin to make sense.[9]

I will assume for the sake of argument (but also from personal conviction) that the experience of watching a film can be a conversion, a *metanoia*, a "radical shift in perspective," and that it is here we ought to open our theological investigation, with our own subjective response. To begin with movies as cultural objects is to put them behind glass, to see them as relics or exhibits in a museum, bodies on a slab prepared for dissection. Proceeding in this manner, theological film criticism

> hinges upon the notion that the critic, director, screenplay writer, or some other creative force behind the film develops a certain theological agenda or concept, and the distinctive goal of the theological critic is to uncover that concept.[10]

This "arm's length" technique proceeds as though theological engagement with film were a form of treasure hunt or academic exercise in deciphering. Instead, I think we should take seriously the claim I made earlier, that alien encounter movies are about ourselves. I do not mean "about ourselves" in a facile, biographical sense, but about ourselves in that they are of our concern. And so we ought to attend carefully to the subjective experience of watching the film, inhabiting and reflecting upon our own affective responses. While this is not an unprecedented departure for theological film criticism, it remains relatively rare. Film theology has tended to limit itself to two strategies, either to mine films for religious "meaning" or to map

---

9. Bevans, *Models of Contextual Theology*, 103; italics original.
10. Martin and Ostwalt, *Screening the Sacred*, 14.

religious messages onto the film. So, for example, Robert Jewett argues for an

> interpretative arch which operates by seeking analogies between ancient and modern texts and situations. I visualise an arch with one end anchored in the ancient world and the other in a contemporary cultural situation.[11]

Larry Kreitzer reverses what he calls the "hermeneutical flow" and argues that "cinematic interpretation may provide us with a helpful doorway through which to enter the hermeneutical arena of New Testament studies."[12] Steve Nolan rightly recognizes the reductive nature of both these approaches, arguing that "religious film criticism has been seduced into a futile pursuit of cinematic analogue."[13] While I do not wish to employ Nolan's favored, Lacanian methodology, I agree with him that the analogue approach is "inappropriate" and "fruitless."[14] Perhaps instead we could adopt Nathaniel Dorsky's concentration on the bodily experience of film, our visceral response. He identifies a concordance between "film and our human metabolism."[15] The language of film, Dorsky argues, is

> a direct and intimate metaphor or model for our being, a model which [has] the potential to be transformative, to be an evocation of the spirit, and to become a form of devotion.[16]

---

11. Jewett, "St. Paul at the Movies," 358.
12. Kreitzer, "New Testament in Fiction," 372.
13. Nolan, "Towards a New Religious Film Criticism," 169.
14. Nolan, "Towards a New Religious Film Criticism," 177.
15. Dorsky, "Devotional Cinema," 407.
16. Dorsky, "Devotional Cinema," 407.

Of course, Dorsky's emphasis on cinema as incitement to transformation is particularly appropriate given our focus here on faith and conversion. But, appealing as Dorsky's devotional approach is, I want to settle on a more poetic, personal, and peculiar way into the films we are watching. So, in the case of *Stalker*, I suggest we take Tarkovsky at his word:

> I had the greatest difficulty in explaining to people that there is no hidden, coded meaning in the film [in this case, *Mirror* (1975), the film Tarkovsky made immediately before *Stalker*], nothing beyond the desire to tell the truth. Often my assurances provoked incredulity and even disappointment. Some people evidently wanted more: they needed arcane symbols, secret meanings. They were not accustomed to the poetics of the cinema image. And I was disappointed in my turn.[17]

For Tarkovsky, cinema is primarily a poetic and a moral medium; it is neither a model nor a metaphor (as Dorsky would have it); it serves no intellectual function; and there is no concept to be "uncovered." It is certainly not a "doorway." Rather, if cinema does have a function, Tarkovsky argues, it is "relating the person to the whole world."[18] More generally still, he maintains, the purpose of all art has been widely misunderstood:

> the allotted function of art is not, as is often assumed, to put across ideas, to propagate thoughts, to serve as example. The aim of art is to prepare a person for death, to plough and

---

17. Tarkovsky, *Sculpting in Time*, 133.
18. Tarkovsky, *Sculpting in Time*, 66.

> harrow his soul, rendering it capable of turning to good.[19]

As works of art, therefore, the two films we are considering, *Stalker* and *Under the Skin*, must have moral and metaphysical roles to play *in our lives* above and beyond any intellectual or ideological or exemplary "message" that may appear to be derivable from them. This explicitly sets us the challenge I defined above: not to uncover a concept or agenda, or to draw analogies or build arches or to see a film as a doorway, but to discern what effect it has on ourselves. This is the approach favored by Robert Johnston, who sensibly urges the Christian moviegoer "to first view a movie on its own terms before entering into theological dialogue with it" and to "let the images themselves suggest meaning and direction."[20]

Johnston's subjective, dialogical approach to theological engagement with film is echoed in Stephen Bevans's transcendental model of contextual theology which we introduced briefly above.[21] As Bevans explains this model, the emphasis is on the subject engaged in theological reflection, rather than on the object of that reflection; the starting point for theology is personal experience.

> Instead of beginning with the conviction that reality is 'out there,' existing somehow independently of human knowing, [the transcendental model] suggests that the knowing subject is intimately involved in determining reality's basic shape.[22]

---

19. Tarkovsky, *Sculpting in Time*, 43.
20. Johnston, "Reel Spirituality," 318.
21. Bevans, *Models of Contextual Theology*, 103–16.
22. Bevans, *Models of Contextual Theology*, 104.

Perfect in Weakness

Bevans argues that theology undertaken in this way is best characterized as process rather than as content. And this process is at once subjective and moral; so it harmonizes interestingly with Tarkovsky's call for art to prepare a person, to harrow the soul. We have found a place, it seems, where theology and art, theology and cinematic art are engaged in close and fruitful dialogue. As we shall see, Bevans's argument that the knowing subject is "involved in determining reality's basic shape" will prove especially valuable in the context of *Stalker*.

We already developed the cliché that alien encounter stories are really ways of encountering ourselves when we argued that these stories also always raise questions and problematics around the notion of faith. This could now do with a little finessing. The question of faith arises because alien encounter stories are always essentially aporetic; they confront us with existential perplexities and confusions. I disagree with J. G. Ballard when he says that science fiction places "some kind of metaphysical and philosophical framework around man's place in the universe."[23] Science fiction is actually concerned with precisely the opposite: problematizing and dismantling accepted metaphysical and philosophical frameworks, pitching us into new predicaments, and thereby triggering a faith response. Like Deckard in Ridley Scott's *Blade Runner* (1982), our lives, even our conceptions of ourselves, are disrupted or demolished by the experience of the "other." Now we have to trust that the outsider, the alien, the other will ultimately take our hand and pull us to safety. Faith.

Stalker concerns us; it faces us with the ultimate *aporia*, the final puzzle—loss of meaning; and it ponders how we respond faithfully when confronted by this loss in our lives. For this reason, I think it is essential to retain the "I"

23. Ballard, *User's Guide to the Millennium*, 204.

at the heart of my reflecting. Like the theologian Dorothy Sölle, I feel that to do otherwise is damagingly inappropriate both to the process of theology and to an appreciation of the film:

> I consider the separation of the personal from the professional, of one's own experience from reflections that then vaunt themselves as "scientific" philosophical-theological thought, to be a fatal male invention, the overcoming of which is a task for any serious theology.[24]

Instead of laying out a systematic methodology from the outset, therefore, I wish to deploy what we might call a "magpie methodology," an appeal to a set of unexpected, unlikely, idiosyncratic texts and artifacts in order to throw stolen or borrowed light on these films' themes and preoccupations. I am less interested in the harsh, bright light of analysis, and drawn more to the flickering "lying" light emerging from the projector's booth.[25] This methodology (if it is a methodology) strikes me as potentially more fruitful than strictly critical and theoretical strategies when it comes to thinking about cinema. In his reflection on presence, Ralph Harper expresses a similar concern and adopts a comparable line of attack:

> I fear the hardening effect of definitions and analysis at a time when we have lost the familiarity with presence both in religion and in ordinary experience. I feel strongly that we must approach presence tentatively, historically, even lyrically.[26]

24. Sölle, *Window of Vulnerability*, 35.

25. "Telling the truth by lying is a way of defining fiction" (Cavell, *World Viewed*, 222). Cavell's thinking about cinema haunts this book as the Wizard's voice haunts Oz.

26. Harper, *On Presence*, 4.

Perfect in Weakness

Surely Harper's methodology with respect to a subject as vague and amorphous as presence cannot helpfully be brought to bear on our current close focus on a particular work of art? I believe it can, and for the reasons Tarkovsky himself gave: we should not be mining films for meaning, but responding to them subjectively, poetically, allowing ourselves to be harrowed.

One further programmatic point: *Stalker* is a film partly about boundaries and borders; more specifically, it is about crossing borders and thereby denying them or negating them. Again, taking *Stalker*'s themes as formal guidelines or prompts toward framing a theological appraisal of the film, I want this notion of crossing boundaries to inform our response, allowing for a permeability between disciplines and contexts. I want to say, by way of proviso, that nowhere will the following discussion be more theological than when it is engaged with cultural, literary, or philosophical ideas. As Alasdair MacIntyre has argued, nothing has been more destructive of research in the humanities than contextualization interpreted as balkanization, as boundary drawing:

> The curriculum has increasingly become one composed of an assorted ragbag of disciplines and subdisciplines, each pursued and taught in relative independence of all the others, and achievement within each consists in the formation of the mind of a dedicated specialist.[27]

The dedicated specialist, the committed contextualist, is bound to see and abide by borders everywhere; the universalist recklessly fails to see borders anywhere. The theologian, whose work begins at a contested border, at a riverbank where blows are exchanged and wounds

27. MacIntyre, *God, Philosophy, Universities*, 173–74.

received,[28] surely recognizes borders, but is called to limp across them again and again in search of blessing, in search always of the borderless, the limitless.

---

28. Gen 32:24–30.

1

CRACKED CISTERNS

> Christ leads me through no darker room
> than he went through before;
> he that into God's Kingdom comes
> must enter by this door.
>
> —RICHARD BAXTER, *POETICAL FRAGMENTS*

Dogged by problems from the start, Andrei Tarkovsky's masterpiece was almost never made. Shooting was scheduled to begin at Isfara, Tajikistan in April of 1977, but these plans had to be abandoned when the area was hit by a violent earthquake. Having relocated to Tallinn in Estonia, filming could commence. But after three months' work, Tarkovsky (1932–86) found that the rushes were poor and the condition of the film stock degraded; furious, he blamed the suppliers of the film stock, he blamed his cameraman for failing to check the quality of the film, and he blamed the technicians at his production company, Mosfilm, for using the wrong development procedures.

Cracked Cisterns

Tarkovsky describes the situation in his diary as a "total disaster."[1] But in disaster, Tarkovsky found the motivation to carry on; in disaster he found redemption:

> [the disaster is] so conclusive that one actually has the sense of a fresh stage, a new step to be taken—and that gives one hope.[2]

This hopeful stepping, as he calls it—out of disaster, out of chaos, out of despair—gives us a hint as to the character, determination, and vision of Tarkovsky the artist. But it also finds full and moving expression in *Stalker*, the film he goes on to make. *Stalker* is shaped and characterized by this movement, a hopeful sense of being impelled toward something better, something elusive yet tangible, something that draws us toward the margins but which is also at the heart of ourselves.

Tarkovsky's fifth film, *Stalker* has the timeless, unsettling atmosphere of a dream, the disjointed and compressed tumbling out of a Dostoevsky novel, the crystalline quality of a fairy story or a Russian folk tale. And like all fairy tales, *Stalker* is ultimately about transformation, or the possibility of transformation. The theme of transformation—or conversion—runs throughout the film in quasi-sacramental modalities—as baptism, as lament, as creation, as redemption. And its element is water.

Water features in almost every scene of *Stalker*—standing in puddles, fast-flowing, falling as rain, dripping, drifting, rippling in a glass, disrupted at the bottom of a well; in one image (the only shot making the final edit from the Tajikistan shoot), the landscape, the ground itself seems to undulate as though everything were water. And water pours through the vast concrete spaces, tunnels, and

1. Tarkovsky, *Time within Time*, 146.
2. Tarkovsky, *Time within Time*, 146.

corroding tanks. It saturates and sacralizes, reclaims an environment that was once human, but is no more:

> For my people have committed two evils: they have forsaken me, the fountain of living water, and dug out cisterns for themselves, cracked cisterns that can hold no water.[3]

We are led through these cracked cisterns and the waters they cannot contain by the Stalker himself, a John the Baptist figure propelled across borders and boundaries into a wilderness, preaching repentance: a new way of being: "Let everything that's been planned come true. Let them believe!"[4]

So the water in *Stalker* is the water of baptism, and the film is ultimately sacramental. In common with sacramental liturgy, the film is thematically structured around transformation, *metanoia*, and conversion. Unlike *Close Encounters*, *Stalker* implicates us, calls for us—as subjects—to risk believing, to risk being changed.

Overlaying these deep sacramental themes are experiences familiar to everyone: love and divided loyalty, hope and despair, running risks and facing failure. The movie's themes of transformation and faith play out both sacramentally and psychologically within an overall metaphysical and cultural context which we could call the "perhaps predicament." *Stalker* is a vivid, relentless, "harrowing" depiction of this predicament.

The "perhaps predicament" is where we live, the air we breathe; it could be characterized as a post-Enlightenment or postmodern condition, but arguably it is more pervasive

[3.] Jer 2:13.
[4.] Tarkovsky, *Stalker*. Unless otherwise specified, all quotes from *Stalker* are from the Curzon Artificial Eye DVD release. See Tarkovsky, *Andrei Tarkovsky: Collected Screenplays* for an earlier draft of the screenplay.

and more fundamental than either of these labels suggest. It is the recognition that, epistemologically and existentially, we are all in something of a tight spot; the world presents itself to us in a way that appears irresolvably ambiguous. Cinema itself becomes a paradigm of the predicament: a presentation of the world to us without at the same time requiring us to be present to the world. Cinema teases us with a taste of transcendence; it is, in essence, an exquisite uncoupling of ourselves from the world. Or that, at least, is its aim. Perhaps it is an unrealizable aim. The fourth cen‑ tury church father Gregory of Nyssa (ca. 335–ca. 395), who will prove a crucial conversation partner throughout our exploration of *Stalker*, would deny the possibility of our ever being able to achieve a genuine uncoupling, true tran‑ scendence. We might say that theater allows us to imitate the *theoi*, but never to join them: we are watching with the groundlings, not from the gods. In his seventh homily on *Ecclesiastes*, Gregory says,

> The whole of creation is unable to stand outside of itself by means of an intuitive knowing grasp, but always remains within itself; and whatever it sees, it sees only itself, and if it believes it sees something beyond itself—well, it is not of its nature to see beyond itself.[5]

With this in mind, the cliché about science fiction al‑ ways being about ourselves can be elevated to a statement concerning the limits of our epistemological capacity:

5. Gregory of Nyssa, *In Ecclesiasten* 7 (*PG* 729B): "Οὕτω καὶ πᾶσα ἡ κτίσις ἔξω ἑαυτῆς γενέσθαι διὰ τῆς καταληπτικῆς θεωρίας οὐ δύναται, ἀλλ' ἐν αὑτῇ μένει ἀεὶ, καὶ ὅπερ ἂν ἴδῃ, ἑαυτὴν βλέπει, κἂν οἰηθεί τι ὑπερ ἑατὴν βλεπειν, το ἐκτὸς ἑαυτῆς φύσιν ἰδεῖν οὐκ ἔχει." (Some of the Greek and Latin texts that follow are obscure, hard to find, and some have no published English translations. As a conse‑ quence, except where indicated, all translations from Greek or Latin are my own. In each case I will quote the original text.)

"Perhaps" – a post-modern
Perfect in Weakness 'Certainty'

> O human beings gazing on the all, recognize . . . your own nature![6]

Cinema, like any art form, can never justify its claim to a privileged transcendent viewpoint. To pretend to hold this viewpoint (as cinema does) can be titillating, but it is actually tragic. Denied access to a super-lunary or divine realm of certainties and principles, we are thrown inevitably back on our devices and desires.

> I am precisely who I am because I exist at this particular point in time, because I am a recipient of a particular national and cultural heritage, because I have a particular set of parents and have received a particular amount and quality of education.[7]

The impossibility of the camera's transcendence, the inescapable specificity of our subjective experience, the prison of the particular returns us to "perhaps."

Where science once guaranteed progress, we now encounter only perhaps; where the church offered truth and the surety of salvation, we now find only perhaps; where political and social ideologies offered answers to deep-rooted social injustices, we now remain incredulous, succumbing to the perhaps. The old verities became versions of a truth that, far from being simple and unchanging, turns out to be culturally determined rather than universally determinative. Perhaps, we now recognize, lies at the root of physics in the form of the Uncertainty Principle; perhaps governs policy-making by eradicating hegemonic claims to cultural, racial, or religious correctitude; perhaps has undermined

---

6. Gregory of Nyssa, *In Ecclesiasten*, 1 (*PG* 625B): ""Ὦ ἄνθροποι, εἰς τὸ πᾶν ἀποβλέποντες, τήν ἑαυτων φύσιν νοήσατε."

7. Bevans, *Models of Contextual Theology*, 104.

authority in all walks of life, not least the church: perhaps emptied the pulpit and the pews.

This is the volatile and insecure late-twentieth-century context into which *Stalker* spoke. And nearly fifty years later, the "perhaps predicament" remains just as pervasive (arguably more so), and *Stalker* still has a great deal to say. No film, in my view, has plumbed the "perhaps predicament," given it shape and depth, as successfully as *Stalker*. For Tarkovsky, I suggest in passing, "perhaps" is a radical, and potentially risky response to the Soviet authority under which he was working. But *Stalker* is much more deeply radical and risky than any perceived political payload. In fact, I will argue, risk is the film's response to the "perhaps predicament." Risk, it suggests, is the ground of faith; risk lies at the root of all creation; risk is the corollary of love. I believe *Stalker*, and the risk-laden ideas to which it gives expression, presents contemporary Christian apologists with a challenge, and an opportunity. It is an opportunity that, were it to be grasped, would bed Christianity back into its apocalyptic, mystical roots. There is a danger of this sounding abstruse, rarefied, and alienating. I hope, however, to show that it is quite the reverse. By applying Stephen Bevans's model of transcendental contextual theology and Gregory of Nyssa's *Ecclesiastes*-inspired reflections on our limited epistemological capacity to *Stalker*, we might begin to see how Christianity could speak more winningly to the generations that have grown up with the "perhaps predicament," and who are, as a consequence, suspicious of all claims to authoritative, objective truth, to definitive answers, to catechisms and formularies. Stephen Bevans argues,

> What the transcendental model [of contextual theology] emphasizes is that every authentic Christian theologizes not by virtue of how much he or she knows or by the accuracy with which

he or she is able to express doctrine. Rather, to
the extent that a person of faith obeys the transcendental precepts . . . in trying to articulate
and deepen his or her faith.[8]

Stalker may not offer any answer to the deep "perhaps" questions that it raises, but it does offer an honest,
authentic, and moving way of engaging with the questions
in a context of faith and doubt, of trying to articulate and
deepen our faith.

Stalker, as I have said, has "perhaps," has *aporia* written all the way through it, like a stick of rock candy. For
Tarkovsky, perhaps is the ground of faith, and faith, it has
been suggested, is the subject of all his films.[9] Faith, as it is
explored in *Stalker*, is depicted less as a defined and codified belief system and more as a function or symptom of
fallibility, a struggle, as praxis: it is demanding, dangerous,
and transgressive. Faith—and the lack of it—transforms
and shapes the lives of the characters. In this sense, *Stalker*
is a cinematic and dramatic realization of Wittgenstein's
assertion that

> the *words* you utter or what you think as you ut-
> ter them are not what matters, so much as the
> difference they make at various points in your
> life. How do I know that two people mean the
> same when each says he believes in God? . . . A
> theology which insists on the use of *certain par-
> ticular* words and phrases, and outlaws others,

---

8. Bevans, *Models of Contextual Theology*, 106.

9. Jolyon Mitchell quotes Tarkovsky as saying that all his films are "about one thing: an extreme manifestation of faith" (Mitchell, "Un-derstanding Religion and Film," 193). In fact, what Tarkovsky said is this: "My first two films are . . . in the final analysis, both about the same thing. They are about the extreme manifestation of loyalty to a moral debt, the struggle for it, and faith in it—even to the extent of a personality crisis" (Tarkovsky, *Andrei Tarkovsky: Interviews*, 33).

> does not make anything clearer (Karl Barth).
> It gesticulates with words, as one might say,
> because it wants to say something and does not
> know how to express it. *Practice* gives the words
> their sense.[10]

Stalker is not about a manifestation of faith, but the fallible practice of faith. What is the relevant difference between a manifestation and a practice? A manifestation, in cinematic terms, remains, as it were, up on the screen, its meaning objectively readable by reference to the niceties and conventions of cinema. *Stalker*, as we shall see, is deliberately transgressive, one might say "transfigurative" of cinematic convention; the locus and status of the screen is constantly called into question. Applying Bevans's model of transcendental theology, and responding to Wittgenstein's emphasis on *practice* and difference, the film's meaning is readable through the subjective, practical difference the film effects in us; its meaning is the *metanoia*, the conversion it triggers in us. When the Stalker prays "Let them believe!," he is praying for us. This implied breaking of the film's two-dimensional plane to include us as elements in a metanarrative is implicit at several points in the film (we will examine some of these moments later). It becomes explicit toward the end of the story, when the Stalker's Wife addresses us directly, appealing to us for corroboration and approval. One way in which *Stalker* dramatically construes what Bevans calls a "change in horizon," a conversion, is the crossing or breaching of borders. Tarkovsky seems to be saying that the journey the characters make in *Stalker* is ultimately our journey of conversion, of transfiguration, if we are prepared to encounter what may defy understanding.

On December 29, 1974, during the planning of *Stalker*, Tarkovsky made the following diary entry in which

10. Wittgenstein, *Culture and Value*, 85e. Wittgenstein's italics.

he outlines in very general terms his aims for the film. He wanted the film to be

> totally harmonious in form: unbroken, detailed action, but balanced by a religious action, entirely on the plane of ideas, almost transcendental, absurd, absolute.[11]

Right from the start, Tarkovsky conceived *Stalker* as a religious act, as praxis, as prayer. With this in mind, let us begin by looking a little more closely at the film itself.

The Stalker, an illegal guide, leaves his Wife and disabled daughter in order to lead two men—the Writer and the Professor—on a dangerous, illicit journey to find a fabled Room in which their deepest desires will be fulfilled, or so the Stalker claims.

This Room lies hidden at the heart of an area of land—the Zone—that has been cordoned off, believed to have been visited by aliens. The human population has been evacuated, and the military now patrol the perimeter. There are reports of strange happenings, supernatural phenomena inside the Zone.

We first meet the Stalker, his Wife, and daughter sleeping in bed together in their apartment by a noisy railway line. The camera pans—studiedly, coolly—across their sleeping faces. And then back. This time the Stalker's eyes are open. Right from the start, Tarkovsky is emphasizing the often imperceptible or blurred border between sleep and wakefulness. This is the first of the borders *Stalker* addresses. The border between sleep and wakefulness stands as a paradigm for all the other borders we will meet and cross during the course of the film: between dream and reality, between detailed action and the transcendental, the

---

11. Tarkovsky, *Time within Time*, 101.

serious and the absurd, the conditional and the absolute, faith and despair.

Having crept out of bed and quietly dressed, the Stalker is confronted by his Wife, who begs him to stay, not to leave her alone again, not to risk everything they have in order to venture back into the Zone. But he refuses to listen, leaves the flat, and meets the Writer and the Professor at a bar. They embark on their mission, approaching the fortified perimeter of the Zone in a jeep. The watchtowers, barbed wire, barriers, and searchlights that mark the entry to the Zone would immediately have reminded a contemporary audience of the border between East and West Germany; it looks like the Berlin Wall. Today it calls to mind the wonderfully misnamed Demilitarized Zone between North and South Korea. The three men somehow manage to evade the troops on a motorized rail trolley which trundles along the tracks, away from the border, and into the Zone.

Up until this point, the film has been shot in a sepia-tinted black and white. As the rhythmic trundling sounds of the trolley become increasingly distorted into an eerie electronic half-music,[12] the film suddenly and inexplicably switches to color. Perhaps this shift from black and white to color marks a physical boundary, an ontological distinction between the "real world" and the Zone. Or perhaps it reflects the changed and heightened psychological state of the characters at this point in the story. Of course, marking out "territory" (geographical or psychological) by shifting between black and white, and color is not an innovation. In this respect, *Stalker* has an obvious if unexpected cinematic antecedent; whether or not Tarkovsky was deliberately

---

12. Eduard Artemyev's score for *Stalker* is a visionary blend of analogue synthesized atmospherics—shimmering, droning, clattering—overlaid with ghostly, melancholy, folk-inflected melodies using traditional instruments: a duduk and an Azerbaijani tar.

Perfect in Weakness

referring to *The Wizard of Oz* (1939) in *Stalker*, the comparison is striking and constructive.[13] As well as using color and black and white to draw distinctions between places, both films are quests through a landscape that is at once mystical and moral. These quests are proscribed and transgressive "ways" to discovery, to self-discovery; both films chart rites of passage. And both end in bathetic revelations that raise more questions than answers.

Once the trolley has stopped in the Zone, the Stalker for the first time appears relaxed and happy. Returning from having briefly reconnoitered the vicinity, he announces to the Writer and the Professor, "We're home!,"[14] a line we might reasonably expect at the end of a journey, not at the outset. We must recognize that we are already in a world turned upside down.

---

13. Geoff Dyer has also referred to the apparent similarities between *Stalker* and *The Wizard of Oz*. He claims these similarities "have been widely remarked on" (Dyer, *Zona*, 57). But he cites no sources and I have not been able to locate any published material drawing the comparison. While Dyer recognizes the programmatic, formal echoes between the films, he does not dig deeper into the shared psychological and spiritual spaces both films (albeit in radically different ways) set out to explore.

14. Tarkovsky, *Stalker*.

2

JOURNEY

> Toto, we're home. Home! And this is my room, and
> you're all here. And I'm not gonna leave here ever,
> ever again, because I love you all, and—oh, Auntie
> Em—there's no place like home!
>
> —Dorothy, *The Wizard of Oz*

Ubi stabilitas, ibi religio.

Where there is stability, there is religion. So said Abbot Lugidus (or Molua), the sixth-century founder of the monastery of Clonfert in Ireland, among many others.[1] For Lugidus, the religious life is rooted, static.[2] If we accept

---

1. *AS*, August 4th, 351.

2. Lugidus's dictum is a concise expression of Benedictine regulation. According to Benedict, "everything necessary ought to be available within the walls of the monastery so that there is no need for the monks to go wandering about outside [*vagandi foras*], which is completely unprofitable for their souls [*omnino non expedit animabus*

Lugidus's statement as normative of religious life, then we must also accept that Tarkovsky is an avowedly irreligious filmmaker:

> The artist seeks to destroy the stability by which society lives, for the sake of drawing closer to the ideal. Society seeks stability, the artist—infinity.[3]

The artist destroys that which makes religion possible. The romantic notion of the iconoclastic and isolated artist was peculiarly potent for Tarkovsky during the tortuously difficult filming of *Stalker*. In a diary entry for May 1977, he says, "Filming is fraught with problems, I don't know how it will work out."[4] The cause of his problems, Tarkovsky is in no doubt, are those around him, his collaborators. "Lightweight, shallow people, with no self-respect. Childish degenerates. Cretins."[5] In other words, society is to blame.

> A person has no need of society, it is society needs him. Society is a defence mechanism, a form of self-protection. Unlike a gregarious animal, a person must live in isolation.[6]

In medieval terms, in Lugidus's terms, to live in isolation, to become unrooted from one's social context is to become a *gyrovagus*, a wanderer, a vagabond.[7] To wander is to err, to be in error. Perhaps it is also to be an artist; it is certainly to take a risk. And risk, as we have already suggested, is a necessary premise of the film's argument, the horizon which defines all of the characters' lives and choices.

---

eorum]" (*Regula*, 66 [*PL* 66:900D]).

3. Tarkovsky, *Sculpting in Time*, 192.
4. Tarkovsky, *Time within Time*, 145.
5. Tarkovsky, *Time within Time*, 145.
6. Tarkovsky, *Time within Time*, 145.
7. Waddell, *Wandering Scholars*, 179.

In fact, risk is a function of choice; to make a choice just is to run a risk. Risk, Tarkovsky seems to suggest in *Stalker*, is the ground of faith and a necessary entailment of being alive; it is what Karl Jaspers termed a *Grenzsituation* or ultimate situation. For Jaspers, these situations are certain, decisive, essential, and related to man's being as such. These ultimate situations are subjectively experienced at the limits of our existence, limits as definitions. Jaspers describes them as

> situations such as the fact that I am always in situations, that I cannot live without conflict and suffering, that I unavoidably incur guilt, that I must die . . . They do not change, except in their appearance; with respect to our existence they are ultimate. They are not surveyable; in our existence we see nothing else behind them. They are like a wall, we come up against, and upon which we founder. They cannot be changed by us, only brought to clarity.[8]

Here, expressed in another way, is Gregory of Nyssa's (and Stephen Bevans's) assertion that we can never step outside of ourselves. In his vast works against the heresies of Eunomius, Gregory writes:

> For all created things are circumscribed within their own limits according to the pleasure of the creator's wisdom.[9]

---

8. Jaspers quoted in Latzel, "Concept of the Ultimate Situation," 188.

9. "τὰ μὲν γὰρ γεγόντα πάντα τοῖς ἰδίοις μέτροις ἐμπεριγεγραμμένα κατὰ τὸ ἀρέσαν τῇ σοφίᾳ τοῦ κτίσαντος" (Gregory of Nyssa, *Contra Eunomium I* [PG 45:365B]). In the *Life of Moses*, Gregory also states "The limits of the boundaries which circumscribe the birds or the fish are obvious: The water is the limit to what swims and the air to what flies" (*Life of Moses*, 2.236).

Perfect in Weakness

To step beyond limitation, the boundary, would be to step outside being: and nature cannot step outside of itself.[10] The real border in *Stalker* is not, therefore, the one marked by a fence and patrolled by guards; it is that natural wall or situation we come up against and cannot cross or overcome.

For the ancient Greeks, the boundary, the margin, was a crucial aspect of their religious beliefs; the border held a special place in their thinking and their worship. They appropriated and incorporated the marginal and the transgressive into their fundamental approach to the world and to the divine. Temples were often sited at the edges of territories, or in isolated, liminal zones. Their god, Hermes, was born at the boundary; his name derives from the piles of stones that marked a border. And yet, at the same time, he is a trickster, the traveler, a messenger, an inveterate crosser of borders.

> The immovable boundary stone is surrounded with tales about the transgression of boundaries and the breaking of taboos through which a new situation, and a new, well-defined order is established.[11]

Burkert's Hegel-inflected analysis of the ancient cult of Hermes seems to suggest that, to the Greeks, the very idea of a border was bound up with transgression. By holding these apparently opposing or antithetical notions in balance, it is possible to bring about or synthesize something new. To cross a border is not to negate or deny it; rather, it is to reconcile divergence, difference, to wrestle with opposition, the other, in an attempt to find a synthesis and to move

---

10. "οὐ γὰρ ἐκβαίνει ἑαυτὴν ἡ φύσις" (Gregory of Nyssa, *de Anima et Resurrection*ε [*PG* 46:141A]).

11. Burkert, *Creation of the Sacred*, 156.

on. Jacob at Peniel is at the border between the human and the divine.[12] He derives his brokenness and his power from being there. In other words, crossing a border is a deeply ambiguous act.

> Smugglers would be lost without frontiers and prohibitions: they are merely the shadows of customs officials.[13]

Paradoxically, to deny the border is to affirm it; as a matter of necessity, transgression is—at least in part—reactionary.

In *Stalker*, we are made aware of the risks involved in crossing the border and venturing into the Zone by the Stalker's Wife, who begs her husband not to go, not to put his life, his freedom, and his family at risk. The Wife gives voice to the *Grenzsituation*: do not cross over, for you may not come back. And if you do come back, the authorities will put you in prison again, have you locked up like the young people listening to the starman on the radio.

This blurring of geography and psychology is typical of *Stalker*: the landscape of the film is defined, bordered, and zoned in the way human existence is defined and bordered by Jaspers's ultimate situations, by Gregory's limits. A life without these situations and limits would not be a human life. Yet the urge to travel out there—over the edges, across the borders—will not be denied. To travel over these borders is to aim for the impossible perspective. The attraction of the border, the margin, the limit, is the impulse of all artistic endeavour. Hermes is the messenger of the gods: like an artist, a starman, he has a message to communicate, a truth gleaned from the margins, the borderlands, from beyond; he is *extra*. The creative urge is the illicit desire to go beyond the limit, to go beyond nature, to see and say

---

12. Gen 32:24–30.
13. Lecercle, *Philosophy through the Looking-Glass*, 193.

something new, and therefore something impossible. Impossible because

> There is nothing new under the sun.
> Is there a thing of which it is said,
> "See this is new?"
> It has already been.[14]

All art is transgressive, aiming to reveal and thereby (impossibly) to overcome this *Grenzsituation*. Arguably, this urge for the border finds its *ne plus ultra*, its most tragic expression, in cinema. Here the border confronts us most visibly, most tangibly, as the screen, the ultimate ontological limit. However hard we try to ignore the screen, penetrate the screen, to disguise it, with all the ingenuity and technology available to us, we can never be Hermes or Jacob; we can never cross the border. And to try to cross it is to try to overcome some limit in ourselves, like a fish trying to live out of the water, or a bird out of the air. The cinema screen is not so much the stage of a fantasy (manifestation), as the revelation of a practical reality: our own limitedness. All cinema is tragedy. Unlike fish or birds, we are painfully, tragically aware of our limit situation, and we feel trapped. The screen reveals this distinctive duality of our own nature. For Gregory of Nyssa, the human being is the only creature which belongs both in the sensible world and in the intelligible: in the stalls and up on the screen. In his commentary on the Psalms, Gregory suggests that the human being itself is a "boundary" or "frontier" (μεθόριος), straddling the border between the sensible and the intelligible realms. And in turning away or abstaining from the earthly, lower, animal nature, the human being approaches the divine realm.[15] By literally

14. Eccl 1:9–1.
15. Gregory of Nyssa, *In Psalmos* 7 (*PG* 44:457B–C).

incorporating the limit, humanity feels bound to transcend it; the breaching of the barrier is effected for Gregory by the glance, by looking, by watching.

> The watching soul, through wonder at those things [creation] appearing, and with an enquiring mind considers the divine intellect, by whose works it is known that it is.[16]

It is in looking, in watching, that the human being is best able to fulfil their unique place in creation: coming to an awareness of God by contemplating God's works. To cross the border from the sensible to the intelligible, to approach the numinous (τὸν νοούμενον), is to turn to God, and by so doing, drawing the whole of creation toward its fulfilment in the eternal kingdom.

For the characters in *Stalker*, illegally crossing the border, Hermes-like or Baptist-like, into the Zone is complex and dangerous; the men have to hide in marshalling yards and alley ways, they have to watch for the right moment, to avoid searchlights and patrolling guards; at one point, they are shot at. This elaborate rigmarole around the crossing of the border serves no plot function; it is simply there to underline the risk that marks the beginning of the adventure, the beginning of any adventure. More than the Zone itself, the border, the boundary, the limit, is the setting of Tarkovsky's film. We are, we feel, journeying inward to the limits of our nature.

---

16. "βλέπουσα ἡ ψυχὴ, διὰ τοῦ θαύματος τῶν φαινομένων, ἀναλογίζεται τῇ διανοίᾳ τὸν διὰ τῶν ἔργων νοούμενον ὅτι ἔστιν" (Gregory of Nyssa, *In Cantica Canticorum Homilia* 11 [*PG* 44:1009D]).

PERFECT IN WEAKNESS

JOURNEY

In the rest of this chapter, I want to consider the possibility that, in *Stalker*, Tarkovsky is drawing on an ancient, scriptural, Christian, and folkloric notion of adventure and of journey. After all, journey lies at the heart of Christian witness from the beginning; immediately following his baptism, the Spirit drives Jesus out into the wilderness,[17] just as God had driven Adam and Eve out of paradise.[18] And in his turn, Jesus sends out the apostles, instructing them "that they should take nothing for their journey, except a mere staff—no bread, no bag, no money in their belt."[19]

Juxtaposing Jesus' life and ministry with Lugidus's claim concerning *stabilitas* appears to reveal a real tension in the way religious life is lived, or ought to be lived. Is it ideally static and stable, or is it ideally dynamic, risky, and unstable? This tension is manifest in *Stalker*'s structure too: a stable, nuclear unit is broken, a home is left, a border crossed, and an adventure embarked upon; then this direction of travel is reversed in homecoming and a moving passage in praise of loyalty and devotion. I intend to look at this structure from a number of angles, but first I briefly want to place these opposing tensions—between the static and the dynamic—in an historical context.

With the collapse of the Roman Empire and the subsequent centuries of tumultuous political and social turmoil, we find, I suggest, the motive force behind Lugidus's assertion, the impetus for seclusion, stasis, and stability. As more stable political and economic structures begin to emerge in Europe, as foreign trade links are established and sovereign alliances forged, a renewed sense of what we might call

17. Mark 1:12; Matt 4:1; Luke 4:1.
18. Gen 3:23–24.
19. Mark 6:7–8.

JOURNEY

"mission" begins to emerge in the social and religious imaginary.[20] The *Ordo Vagorum* and the mendicant orders are founded in the twelfth century with the primary purpose of going out, of evangelization;[21] pilgrimage becomes popular; the Crusades bloodily inaugurate a new and ambitious era of pan-European dynamism. At the same time, and as a direct result of these changes, the literary genre of the "quest" develops and evolves out of the older *chanson des gestes*, lyrical accounts of valiant deeds. Where the notion of "quest" is largely absent, say, from the *Chanson de Roland* (ca. 1040, but relating a story from the eighth century) it is absolutely foregrounded in the Arthurian romances of Chrétien de Troyes (1130–91). The Knight evolves from the doer of deeds into the seeker after truth.

In his narrative poem, *Yvain, The Knight of the Lion*, Chrétien describes a world of journeying solitary knights. So the knight, Calogrenant, describes to King Arthur's knights assembled at the Round Table how he took "a path to the right"[22] and entered a dense forest full of brambles, eventually emerging from the forest into Brocéliande, a legendary, enchanted region with a castle, a beautiful maiden, and a magic spring, a place which is also the location of Merlin's tomb.

---

20. Still the best general overview of this period is, in my opinion, Richard Southern's *The Making of the Middle Ages*. Philippe Wolff describes the dawning of "a way of life which was characterized by a liking for risks, the pursuit of gain and the demand for political freedom. It acted like yeast in the blood of a hitherto static society" (Wolff, *Awakening of Europe*, 201).

21. See Waddell, *Wandering Scholars*, 177–213.

22. Chrétien de Troyes, *Arthurian Romances*, 297.

35

Perfect in Weakness

BROCÉLIANDE

Chrétien's depiction of Brocéliande has all the mysterious qualities of fairy tale. Its geographical location is uncertain, and when the knight, Yvain, follows in Calogrenant's footsteps seven years later, he finds Brocéliande exactly as Calogrenant described it, down to the most minute details; time appears not to have passed. In *Mimesis*, his masterly survey of the rise of realism in European literature, Eric Auerbach describes Chrétien's Brocéliande:

> The landscape is the enchanted landscape of fairy tale; we are surrounded by mystery, by secret murmurings and whispers . . . all the things of fairyland; each time they appear before us as though sprung from the ground; their geographical relation to the known world, their sociological and economic foundations, remain unexplained. Even their ethical or symbolic significance can rarely be ascertained with anything approaching certainty. Has the adventure any hidden meaning?[23]

I suggest Brocéliande can be seen as a literary prototype of Tarkovsky's Zone. Even the apparently wilful withholding of clues as to meaning or symbolic significance rings true with Tarkovsky's poetics. Whether or not Tarkovsky or the Strugatsky brothers (who wrote the original short story on which *Stalker* is based and the screenplay for the film itself) were consciously inspired by medieval quest literature is immaterial; the quest trope survives and thrives, as I have suggested, in European folklore, in fairy tale, and in popular films like *The Wizard of Oz*. So, while it is perfectly possible (likely) that Tarkovsky and the Strugatskys were unaware of the taproot (medieval Romance

23. Auerbach, *Mimesis*, 130.

literature), it is almost impossible that they were unaware of its many branches, the folkloric and fairy-tale echoes in the Stalker's quest.

Instead of castles and forests, we find in the Zone a postindustrial wasteland through which our adventurers must travel. But the lack of certainty, the mysteriousness, the suggested spatiotemporal anomalies, the suspicion of magic, of "hidden meaning," all remain unaltered. In Brocéliande, as in the Zone, the landscape—castles, forests, and magic springs in the former; cisterns, crumbling factories, and rusting armaments in the latter—serves as a proving ground, a psychological as much as a physical landscape. So, the Stalker describes the Zone to his companions as

> a highly complex system . . . of traps, as it were, and all of them are deadly. I don't know what happens here when we've gone . . . but people have only to appear for the whole thing to be triggered into motion. Our moods, our thoughts, our emotions, our feelings can bring about change here. And we are in no condition to comprehend them. Old traps vanish, new ones take their place; the old safe places become impassable, and the route can be either plain and easy, or impossibly confusing. That's how the Zone is. It may even seem capricious.[24]

Similarly, and according to Auerbach, Brocéliande

> contains nothing but the requisites of adventure. Nothing is found in it which is not either accessory or preparatory to an adventure. It is a world specifically created and designed to give the knight opportunity to prove himself. So Calogrenant rides all day and encounters nothing but a castle prepared to receive him. Nothing is

24. Tarkovsky, *Andrei Tarkovsky: Collected Screenplays*, 395.

said about all the practical conditions and circumstances necessary to render the existence of such a castle in absolute solitude both possible and compatible with ordinary experience.[25]

The likenesses are obvious—the ultimate incomprehensibility of the place, its apparent purposiveness, the air of expectancy and danger, of waiting traps. More than anything, both Brocéliande and the Zone resemble film sets: performance spaces, stages for the playing out of an adventure. The extent to which *Stalker* is, at least partially, about film-making specifically, and artistic creation in general, is moot and will be discussed in the next chapter. For now, it suffices to say that the Zone and Brocéliande—*like cinema itself*—call our commonly held conceptions of reality into doubt: phenomenal appearances can no longer be counted upon as reliable guides to reality. The camera can lie, a screen can be a veil. Indeed, lying and veiling are of their essence.

But there are also telling mismatches between Brocéliande and the Zone. Chrétien's fairyland is a function of the tale's objective, namely the proving of the knight. In Auerbach's words, it is "created and designed" for a purpose. The creator and designer is clearly Chrétien himself working (albeit brilliantly) to a strictly codified courtly formula. By contrast, Tarkovsky's Zone is not so much a landscape to be moved through as a character to be wrestled with; it is enmeshed in the drama. Where Chrétien's fairyland is fixed and absolute, Tarkovsky's Zone is capricious and various. And yet, the disparity perhaps masks a deeper symmetry. What Auerbach recognizes in Chrétien, Deleuze similarly recognises in Tarkovsky, namely, the crystalline. Just as th physical environment in the courtly romance seems to have no roots in an economic, geographical, or political reality,

---

25. Auerbach, *Mimesis*, 136.

but instead springs, as it were, spontaneously, timelessly into being, so the landscape of *Stalker* is also apparently discontinuous with reality.

> There are cyrstallized spaces [in Tarkovsky's films], when the landscapes become hallucinatory . . . Now what characterizes these spaces is that their nature cannot be explained in a simply spatial way. They imply non-localizable relations.[26]

And for both the knight on the chivalrous quest and the Stalker and his companions, the environment through which they travel is "a series of adventures raised to the status of a fated and graduated test of election."[27]

So, while retaining elements of the narrative structure of the courtly romance, Tarkovsky has chosen to present this quest in a more complex, ambivalent environment. By, as it were, giving the Zone a character, he calls into question the ontological status of the landscape itself in a way that Chrétien does not. For Chrétien, Brocéliande is functional, and its function is determined by the literary conventions within which he is writing. For Tarkovsky, the Zone is not so much functional as expressive (the difference again between manifestation and practice); it is not the manipulable tool of the storyteller, but the story telling itself. And here we find ourselves well and truly through the looking-glass, in the realm of Deleuzian *délire*. Jean-Jacques Lecercle defines *délire* as a form of discourse that lies at the border between sense and nonsense, the peculiarity of which "does not reside in its lack of meaning, but in its surfeit of it."[28] In *délire*, the meaning of a text or utterance is excessive, ob-

26. Deleuze, *Cinema II*, 125.
27. Auerbach, *Mimesis*, 136.
28. Lecercle, *Philosophy through the Looking-Glass*, 3.

truding beyond the intentions of the writer or speaker; it is a "threat to and a substratum of the linguistic structure";[29] it accounts for "the demise of the author as the sole source of textual meaning."[30] *Délire* is disruptive, protean; it

> pervades the text, dissolves the subject, threatens to engulf the reader in its disaster.[31]

We are inevitably reminded of Tarkovsky's own characterization of the filming of *Stalker* as "disaster," and of Susan Sontag's seeing "disaster" as the real subject of science-fiction.[32] The Zone stands in relation to the world from which it is segregated as *délire* stands to the language which it dissolves and threatens and disrupts, and of which it is also the substratum. Both the Zone and *délire* are hived off from the world-language "proper." Both are seen as dangerous, aberrant; they could be empty, or they could be surfeit. Hence the need for borders.

> If the problem of the establishment of frontiers [between what can and cannot be said in a language] becomes crucial, it also means that language will always try to utter what cannot be said, the subject will always be tempted to go beyond the frontier: in order to define a boundary one must at least attempt to cross it. This is exactly what happens in *délire*.[33]

Here, transposed to literature and the philosophy of language, is a group of adventurers, familiar enough to us by now, attempting to cross a border: Jacob, Hermes, Yvain,

---

29. Lecercle, *Philosophy through the Looking-Glass*, 107.
30. Lecercle, *Philosophy through the Looking-Glass*, 37.
31. Lecercle, *Philosophy through the Looking-Glass*, 45.
32. Sontag, "Imagination of Disaster," 209–25.
33. Lecercle, *Philosophy through the Looking-Glass*, 51.

Dorothy, and the Stalker. By crossing that border, that limit, they deny it, and acknowledge it.

In the context of *délire*, the Zone becomes the unspeakable, the unsayable that lies both beyond meaning and somehow underlies it. Perhaps, the Zone suggests, the sayable is defined by the unsayable, sense by nonsense; the "real world" is defined by the Zone—rather than *vice versa*. Reality is defined by mystery. *Stabilitas* and certainty collapse into the ambiguous, into perhaps. Limit situations are defined by the limitless, not by the limited.

LA MANCHA

By the sixteenth century, Brocéliande has become La Mancha, and the heroic, questing knight is now a delusional fantasist, a knight, we are told, who has lost his wits through reading.

> He filled his mind with all that he read, with enchantments, quarrels, battles, challenges, wounds, wooings, loves, torments and other impossible nonsense; and so deeply did he steep his imagination in the belief that all the fanciful stuff he read was true, that to his mind no history in the world was more authentic.[34]

The modern mind has lost faith in the fairy tale. It relegates Brocéliande to "nonsense," to "fanciful stuff," to the muddled, delirious wits of an old man, while we remain in no doubt as to the reality of the situation. We are told that Don Quixote

> had utterly wrecked his reason and fallen into the strangest fancy that ever a madman had in the whole world. He thought it fit and proper . . . to

34. Cervantes, *Don Quixote*, 32.

> turn knight errant and travel through the world
> with horse and armour in search of adventures.[35]

He is a knight errant in both senses of the word. We know it because we are told it. We are not the subjects of delusion, Quixote is. And therein lies the fun, and the pathos.

So, is the Stalker a Quixote figure? We cannot be sure. There is no one, no Cervantes, no Spielberg to tell us one way or the other. The Stalker is our guide. Tarkovsky tantalizes us with references to aliens and meteorites, teases us with contemporary science-fiction tropes, but fails to deliver them, leaving us wondering, wandering, erring. The Zone is adrift: neither medieval nor modern, neither fantasy nor reality, neither here nor there (Deleuze's non-localizable relations).

Chrétien's Brocéliande serves the purpose of the teller of the tale, and Cervantes's joke is to set a fantasy walking through reality; the Zone appears to be the opposite: it seems to serve no purpose, and it feels more as though reality—in the form of the Professor and the Writer—is walking through a fantasy. In other words, *Stalker* seems to suggest, the locus of this modern knightly quest is ourselves. And here Bevans's model comes into its own:

> One needs to begin one's quest for knowing what "is" by attending to the dynamic of one's own consciousness and irrepressible desire to know.[36]

Note how easily Bevans's transcendental model borrows wholesale the sorts of language we have already encountered: quest, dynamic, and desire. Where Bevans chooses to focus on contemporary examples of subjective-transcendental theology, particularly in the work of

---

35. Cervantes, *Don Quixote*, 33.
36. Bevans, *Models of Contextual Theology*, 104.

Bernard Lonergan and Sallie McFague,[37] I want to press on into the landscape, as it were, continuing to expose the historical-cultural roots of this association between subjective consciousness and physical environment.

SINAI

In his *Life of Moses*, Gregory of Nyssa describes the journey of Moses toward the perfection of God. For Gregory, this ascent is metaphorically represented in scripture by Moses's climbing of Mount Sinai.

> He continually climbed to the step above and never ceased to rise higher, because he always found a step higher than the one he had attained.[38]

Gregory uses landscape to represent psychological possibility. The finite landscape—and Moses's journey through it—becomes an analogue for his striving toward perfection, toward God. And paradox inevitably lies at the heart of this analogue because landscape is limited, determinate, whereas God, that toward which Moses is striving, is limitless and absolutely undetermined;[39] the journey must be endless, and therefore—in a sense—fruitless.

> The true vision of God consists . . . in this, that the one who looks up to God never ceases in that desire. What Moses yearned for is satisfied by the very things which leave his desire unsatisfied.[40]

37. Bevans, *Models of Contextual Theology*, 103–5, 110–13.

38. Gregory of Nyssa, *Life of Moses* 2.227.

39. "The one limit of virtue is the absence of limit." Gregory of Nyssa, *Life of Moses* 1.8.

40. Gregory of Nyssa, *Life of Moses* 2.233–35.

Gregory is fascinated by God's saying to Moses, "Here is a place beside me."[41] How, Gregory wonders, can there be a place beside the placeless? "For to something unquantitative [God] there is no measure."[42] Remember that, for Gregory, a human being is limit or boundary (μεθόριος), while God is

> that which penetrates all, and is in all, and contains all, and is circumscribed [περιειργόμενον] by none of the things that are, has no place to which to pass since nothing is devoid of the fullness of God [οὐκ ἔχει ὅπου μεταχωρήσει τῷ μηδὲν εἶναι κενὸν τοῦ θείου πληρώματος].[43]

Gregory's solution to the dilemma lies in a spiritual, analogical reading of the Exodus text: the mountain is to be read as a symbol of the unlimited, unmeasured, and infinite. He has God say the following words to Moses:

> Your desire for what is still to come has expanded and you have not reached satisfaction in your progress and whereas you do not see any limit to the Good, but your yearning always looks for more, the place with me is so great that the one running in it is never able to cease from his progress.[44]

---

41. Exod 33:21.

42. Gregory of Nyssa, *Life of Moses* 2.242.

43. Gregory of Nyssa, *Contra Eunomium* 12.1 (*PG* 45:885C–D). Compare the following passage: "ἁπλοῦς ὁ Θεὸς τῇ φύσει, καὶ ἄϋλος, ἀποιός τε καὶ ἀμεγέθης, καὶ ἀσύνθετος, καὶ τῆς κατὰ τὸ σχῆμα περιγραφῆς ἀλλοτρίως," or "God is simplex by nature, immaterial, without quantity or size, uncomposed and completely without circumscription by shape" (Gregory of Nyssa, *de Hominis Opificio* 23 [*PG* 44:209D]).

44. Gregory of Nyssa, *Life of Moses* 2.242.

JOURNEY

Gregory returns to this theme in his commentary on the *Song of Songs*; it is our duty, he states there, "always to rise up, drawing nearer and nearer along the way, and never ceasing."[45] The "place with me" is categorically not measured or limited or confined within the walls of the monastery in the same way that *délire* will not be measured or limited or confined by a language; it is not *stabilitas*; it is surfeit. I suggest this dynamic, protean "place with me" through which we are called to run and never cease from running finds a modern articulation in Tarkovsky's Zone—a hallowed place, a place beyond borders that elicits yearning, that ultimately withholds satisfaction, and that appears to embody some moral purpose that is somehow part of our own nature.

In chapter 3, I will examine this place or placelessness itself, but here I want to continue to explore the notion of our journeying through, our "quest for knowing what is."[46]

In recent years, there has been a renewed emphasis on the language of journey in relation to faith. The tendency has been to view this journey as having religious faith as the destination; it is a journey *to* faith. In the sorts of journeys we have been looking at, however, in Chrétien of Troyes, in Cervantes, and in Gregory of Nyssa, the notion of "journey" is importantly different. Here it is the journey itself that matters; the destination is either immaterial or unreachable. The point of the journey is the change, the transformation, the conversion that it engenders in the journeyer, in the transcendental subject. For Yvain and Calogrenant, taking "the path to the right" is constitutive of their role and character as knights; for Moses (according to Gregory), his life is a

---

45. "ἀεί τε γὰρ ἐγείρεσθαι χρὴ καὶ μηδέποτε διὰ τοῦ δρόμου προσεγγίζοντας παύσασθαι" (Gregory of Nyssa, *In Cantica Canticorum Homilia* 5 [*PG* 44:876C]).

46. Bevans, *Models of Contextual Theology*, 104.

sequence of events and actions along a path, an eternal path toward unachievable perfection. In other words, these journeys do not appear to be aimed at geographically specified endpoints. Rather the quest has become a means of embedding the notion of subjective transformation or conversion in a dramatic narrative form.

At first glance, the situation in *Stalker* is slightly different. As far as the characters are concerned, there certainly is an endpoint, a goal toward which they are all journeying—the Room, and the fulfillment of their deepest desires. They are like pilgrims hoping for healing, forgiveness, or divine guidance at a holy shrine. As we shall see, however, they are ultimately to be frustrated. Perhaps they ought to have seen themselves not on a pilgrimage, but on a journey, or even an adventure. The difference is clearly teleological, and it has a crucial bearing on how we use and hear "journey" language in a contemporary faith context. As Joanna Collicutt has recently recognized, for many, this language will be used to describe a simple journey to faith:

> The life of faith involves goal-*directed* behaviour; it has a route and destination. So one way of understanding growth [in Christian life and faith] is as progress along the route and towards the destination.[47]

Later, Collicutt elaborates on the notion of journey, and appears to reconsider what a destination in this context might actually be. She focuses on the descriptions of journeys in the gospels.

> These journeys [in the gospel narratives] are very rarely in a straight line; they are full of diversions, there is often some backtracking and,

47. Collicutt, *Psychology of Christian Character Formation*, 77. Collicutt's italics.

as in the journey to Emmaus, the destination sometimes changes. A key feature of many of these journeys is turning or returning.[48]

This is a crucial insight, and it points toward the notion I am wanting to develop here: the journey itself, the turning or returning, *is* the destination inasmuch as it fulfills the transcendental function of the narrative. What I think Gregory of Nyssa is describing in his *Life of Moses*, what Tarkovsky appears to be suggesting in *Stalker*, perhaps what the writers of the gospels imply by the use of journeying in the Jesus narratives, is that faith is itself a journey of endless transformation; it is an adventure. What does this mean in terms of the contemporary language of discipleship? For a start, it means an abandonment of the teleological, pilgrimage approach; there is no end to this journey, no Room waiting for us at the heart of the Zone, no definitive answer. This is not as bleak as it sounds; in fact, as I shall try to show, it is a blessing.

Reflecting on Gregory of Nyssa's *Life of Moses* presents us with an opportunity to read the Stalker's journey spiritually, not just as a timeworn literary topos. For Gregory, a journey is not so much something we make as a function of what we are. Gregory's thought world is structured around Judeo-Christian ideas of the fall and the resurrection, of "turning and returning," as Collicutt puts it. These concepts, as well as being inheritances from Hebrew scripture, are also informed by Hellenic metaphysical notions of procession and return. For Gregory and his fellow Christian Neoplatonists, these ideas can be mapped on to one another, and journey is the key. Let us take the Hellenic ideas first.

Gregory's cosmology and theology are close cousins to the metaphysics of his pagan near-contemporary, Plotinus.

---

48. Collicutt, *Psychology of Christian Character Formation*, 79.

> Standing before all things, there must exist a Simplex, differing from all its sequel, self-gathered not interblended with the forms that rise from it, and yet able in some mode of its own to be present to those others.[49]

According to Plotinus, creation is an endless causal procession from the radically simple into the complexity of the material cosmos which yet retains a relation (of cause and effect, of presence, of belonging) with the simple and unchanging One to which it strives to return. Compare this to Gregory's definition of God as "that which is always the same, neither increasing nor diminishing, immutable to all change whether to better or to worse ... standing in need of nothing else, alone desirable, participated in by all but not lessened by their participation—this is truly real Being."[50] Furthermore, that which is

> without size cannot be calculated, that without form cannot be examined, the incorporeal cannot be measured, that without boundaries cannot be estimated, the inestimable does not admit of more or less.[51]

So, in Gregory we find Plotinus's simplicity/complexity language translated into a schema that compares the

---

49. Plotinus, *Enn.* 5.4.1. I am quoting Stephen Mackenna's translation of the *Enneads* out of personal preference. One of the greatest prose stylists of the early twentieth century (of any century, for that matter), Mackenna is also a deeply Tarkovskian character: melancholy, eccentric, and driven by something other-worldly, a real-life Stalker. See Dodds, *Journals and Letters of Stephen Mackenna*, which also contains Dodds's moving memoir of his friend.

50. Gregory of Nyssa, *Life of Moses* 2.25.

51. "Τὸ ἄποσον οὐ μετερεῖται· τὸ ἀειδὲς οὐ δοκιμάζεται· τὸ ασώματον οὐ σταθμίζεται· τὸ ἀόριστον οὐ συγκρίνεται· τὸ μὴ συγκρινόμενον τοῦ πλείονος καὶ ἐλάττονος οὐκ ἐπιδέχεται λόγον" (Gregory of Nyssa, *In Suam Ordinationem* [PG 46:552B]).

measureless to the measured. For Gregory, ideas of measure, of interval and spacing are fundamental, delimiting created existence.[52]

> The perfection of everything which can be measured by the senses is marked off by certain definite boundaries.[53]

Remember Gregory's description of the air and water as the boundaries or limits for birds or fish. Here he talks of these boundaries or limits as perfections. Everything has its own perfection in the borders and limits of its existence. That which can be measured by the senses belongs to the sensible world, and everything that belongs in the sensible world has its measurable limit, its natural perfection. A human being, as we have already seen, contains within itself the boundary between the sensible and the intelligible worlds. Gregory conceives the ideal human life, therefore, not as a stripping away or simplification in the manner of Plotinus, but as a quest, an ascent, a growing toward the measureless, the limitless, the borderless, always trying to break free of its limit situations.

This Neoplatonic notion of procession from simplicity to complexity, from the measureless to the measured, is best articulated, to my mind, by the ninth-century philosopher John Scottus Eriugena, who introduced many of these ideas to the Latin west. In the preface to his glosses to the *Ambigua* of Maximus the Confessor (ca. 580–662), Eriugena tells us

> what sort of thing Procession is, namely a multiplication of the divine goodness through all the things that are, descending from the highest to the lowest, firstly from the general essence of all

---

52. See Balthasar, *Presence and Thought*, 27–37.
53. Gregory of Nyssa, *Life of Moses* 1.5.

PERFECT IN WEAKNESS

things, then through the most general genera, next through the more general genera, then the more specific species to the most specific species through differences and properties.[54]

In the fifth book of the *de Divisione Naturae*, Eriugena's magisterial work (incontestably the greatest work of philosophy of the so-called "dark" ages), Eriugena is also able to provide an illustration of how this Neoplatonic metaphysics can be translated into the Christian doctrine of the fall:

> So now this is the man I see, driven out of Paradise; from blessed to wretched; from rich to needy; from eternal to temporal; from vital to mortal; from wise to stupid; from spiritual to animal; from heavenly to mundane; from new to old; from happy to sad; from saved to lost; from the prudent son to the prodigal; straying [*errantem*] from the flock of heavenly virtues, and I grieve for him.[55]

The trajectory exemplified in this passage could serve as a model—or a half-model—for the life of the Stalker in Tarkovsky's film. He is wretched, temporal, mortal, stupid,

---

54. "*Qualis sit processio, id est, multiplicatio divinae bonitatis per omnia, quae sunt, a summo usque deorsum, per generalem omnium essentiam primo, deinceps per genera generalissima, deinde per genera generaliora, inde per species specialores usque ad species specialissimas per differentias proprietatesque descendens.*" (Eriugena, *Praefatio Joannis Scoti versio Ambigorum S. Maximi* [PL 122:1195B]).

55. "*Nunc ergo, hoc est, iam de paradiso expulsum hominem video, factumque de beato miserum, de copioso egenum, de aeterno temporalem, de vitali mortalem, de sapiente stultum, de spirituali animalem, de caelesti terrenum, de novo inveteratum, de laeto tristem, de salvo perditum, de prudentii filio prodigum, ex virtutum caelestium grege errantem, eique condoleo*" (Eriugena, *De Divisione Naturae* 5 [PL 122:862B]).

sad, lost, and straying. Straying is his *métier*; it is all he knows. But, as I say, this is only a half-model; it takes us only so far on the journey, because it lacks the impulse, the yearning to return so movingly depicted in Tarkovsky's *Stalker*. Paul Tillich expresses this as yearning for that "to which one essentially belongs and from which one is existentially separated."[56] This is pure Gregory of Nyssa. We are that which belongs; we have become that which is separated. This tragic dichotomy is the motor of our lives; it is the boundary within us, and the *Grenzsituation* we face. So Eriugena continues his gloss on Maximus by describing how all things in their infinite and complex variety revert, or long to revert, to their single and simple cause:

> And [Maximus describes] likewise, what sort of a good, or manifestly divine thing this reversion might be: a congregation, through the same stages, from the infinite and multiplex variety of those things that are, to the simplest unity of all things, which is in God and is God; so that God might be all things, and all things might be God.[57]

Eriugena's claim that "all things might be God" is clearly Pauline; he is quoting or paraphrasing 1 Corinthians 15:28: "then the Son himself will be made subject to him who put everything under him, so that God may be all in all." This creative model of procession and reversion of the fall and resurrection is clearly dynamic in nature. The

---

56. Tillich, *Dynamics of Faith*, 112.

57. "*Et iterum, eiusdem, divinae videlicet, bonitatis qualis sit reversio id est, congregatio per eosdem gradus ab infinita eorum quae sunt, variaque multiplicatione usque ad simplicissimam omnium unitatem, quae in Deo est et Deus est; ita ut et Deus omnia sit, et omnia Deus sint.*" (Eriugena, *Praefatio Joannis Scoti versio Ambigorum S. Maximi* [*PL* 122:1195B–C]).

twin movement—the fro and to of Neoplatonic metaphysics and their outworking in Christian eschatology is, for the mystically-minded, the dialectical throb of creation itself, "the diastole-systole which is the life of the universe."[58]

It follows that a religion that finds expression only in *stabilitas* may quickly prove stagnant or even stillborn. It is the endless stirring of the waters, the outward movement—from cause into effect, and then back from complex material effects into simple and spiritual causes, and ultimately into the single Cause of all—that gives this model its circular, dynamic quality.

> For us there is one God, the Father, from whom are all things, and for whom we exist.[59]

The plot of *Stalker*, I suggest, mirrors this circular, back and forth movement. And the mirroring is no narrative accident or borrowed trope; it is an expression (the clearest in all of Tarkovsky's films) of his core creative conviction that

> the fate of the genius in the system of human knowledge is amazing and instructive. These sufferers chosen by God, doomed to destroy in the name of movement and reconstruction, find themselves in a paradoxical state of unstable equilibrium between a longing for happiness and the conviction that happiness, as a feasible reality or state, does not exist.[60]

This passage is doubly illuminating. Firstly, of course, it is self-illuminating, as far as Tarkovsky is concerned. Although the context of this passage is a discussion on Spanish art, with Tarkovsky singling out El Greco, Cervantes, and Goya as the archetypal geniuses, it is impossible not

58. Dodds, *Proclus*, 219.
59. 1 Cor 8:6.
60. Tarkovsky, *Sculpting in Time*, 53.

to relate the reference to the genius, chosen by God and therefore doomed to suffer, to the diary entries in which Tarkovsky clearly presents himself (to himself) as the sole, tortured bearer of creative responsibility, as the artist whose role it is to destroy the stability of comfortable society.

Secondly, I think it is illuminating to compare the "paradoxical" state of the genius, poised between a yearning for happiness, and the conviction that this happiness does not exist. Here, in a nutshell, is the predicament of the Stalker, and the plot of his eponymous film. The happiness which the genius is doomed to seek, while always suspecting that it may not exist, is clearly synonymous with the Room at the heart of the Zone, the fulfilment of your deepest desires. It is also the story of Gregory's Moses, never able to cease in his progress toward the unattainable. It is to the unattainable that we must now turn our own attention.

3

THE KINGDOM OF GOD

Toto, I've a feeling we're not in Kansas anymore.

—Dorothy, *The Wizard of Oz*

Perhaps because of its Neoplatonic structure, the plot of *Stalker* is deceptively simple. In short, some men go off in search of something, they do not find it, and they come home. The end. *Stalker* is, in essence, a shaggy dog story, or a wild goose chase. Yet it has been labeled recondite, elusive. Žižek accuses Tarkovsky in *Stalker* of "religious obscurantism."[1] In order to defend *Stalker* from these charges, I want to take a different approach in this chapter, an approach which effectively takes Tarkovsky's film at face value. I want to think of *Stalker* as an absurdist, ludic work with the structure of a joke. Remember, Tarkovsky himself conceived *Stalker* as "absurd."[2]

---

1. Fiennes, *Pervert's Guide to the Cinema*.
2. Tarkovsky, *Time within Time*, 101.

The Kingdom of God

Neoplatonist Renaissance thinkers, like Marsilio Ficino (1433–99), Nicholas Cusanus (1401–64), and Achille Bocchi (1488–1562) used the term *serio ludere* to pick out a mode of philosophical or literary discourse that uses the joke to bring to light essential contradictions and paradoxes in our attempts to understand the nature of God. So, Cusanus published a work entitled *De Ludo Globi*. And Bocchi's five-volume masterpiece is called, catchily, *Symbolicarum Quaestiones, de Universo Genere, quas serio ludebat*.

In fact, *serio ludere* stands as an early modern example of the methodology I am using here, bringing apparently unrelated or unexpected, even unhelpful, fragments and ideas into juxtaposition in order to reveal the contours of the impossible, the ungraspable.[3] So, it is in the spirit of Cusanus's *serio ludere* that I think we should examine *Stalker*.

At the beginning of the film, we are presented with an ominous "report" from a fictitious Professor Wallace, a Nobel laureate, who describes how the Zone came into existence.

> Was it a meteorite? A visit of inhabitants from the cosmic abyss? One way or another our small country has seen the birth of a miracle—the Zone. We immediately sent troops there. They haven't come back. Then we surrounded the

---

3. David Tracy also notes Nicholas Cusanus's use of fragments, and draws attention to his "pluralistic sensibility, his mysticism of limit, his explosion of all scholasticism by articulating the distinct great modern notion of infinity as glimpsed in his retrieval of certain fragments of Ekhart and Dionysius" (Tracy, "Fragments," 180). Tracy recognizes in Cusanus what we have recognized in Gregory of Nyssa: it is not our finitude that (negatively) defines our limits, but that finitude half-perceived in relation to the infinite measurelessness for which we yearn.

Zone with police cordons. Perhaps that was the right thing to do, but I don't know.[4]

And yet, when we cross the border into this place, there is nothing remarkable about it at all. There is, perhaps, a *Marie Celeste* quality to its pervading air of abandonment, but nothing to suggest a supernatural or alien presence, no sign of cataclysm or wholesale destruction, only neglect. The landscape remains partially industrial, albeit marginally more ruinous and overgrown than the landscape we have glimpsed already in the scenes of the Stalker's home and its environs. Meteorites? Cosmic abyss? A miracle? Is this a joke? We are tempted to say, with Ronnie Neary in *Close Encounters*, "No, they're not for real!"

It is worth reflecting on the choice of landscape Tarkovsky made for *Stalker*. His original setting for the Zone, as we have already noted, had been in Isfara, Tajikistan. Isfara would have given us a desert Zone almost completely empty and bare of vegetation, featureless. It is easy to imagine Tarkovsky choosing this location because of its cultural resonances: this is Sinai, the Egyptian desert, the wilderness where Jesus was tempted by Satan; it is a harrowing, empty, unwelcoming place, stripped and desolate. It is the traditional (even scriptural) place of encounter with God:

> The apophatic tradition, despite its distrust of all images about God, makes an exception in using the imagery of threatening places as a way of challenging the ego and leaving one at a loss for words. If we cannot know God's essence, we can stand in God's place—on the high mountain, in the lonely desert.[5]

---

4. Tarkovsky, *Stalker*.
5. Lane, *Solace of Fierce Landscapes*, 65.

The Kingdom of God

Because of the 1977 earthquake, Tarkovsky had to abandon filming in Isfara. There must have been practical and prosaic reasons for the decision; insurance costs would surely have been a factor. It has been suggested by Robert Bird that Tarkovsky came to see this upset as serendipitous, that the director preferred the richer palette of tones that Estonia offered over Tajikistan.[6] I have no doubt that Tarkovsky could have made a desert Zone as mysterious and beautiful and haunting as he was able to with the Estonian version. I do not believe Tarkovsky's decision to move the Zone from the desert to a temperate, northern, postindustrial landscape was simply aesthetic. Instead, I believe he came to see the Isfaran version of the Zone as too "other," too fierce, too scriptural, too expressive of the cliché underlying Lane's description of "threatening places." The Isfaran Zone spoke too obviously into the apophatic romanticism of desert "scenery."[7] In Isfara, it would have been all too easy to believe the Stalker's claims; we would have had no doubt that aliens had visited here, or that some cosmic calamity had occurred, that the landscape itself was somehow burdened with the supernatural. We might expect at any moment to discover the missing World War II squadron of aeroplanes mysteriously relocated to the Sonoran desert in Mexico in *Close Encounters*.

In other words, the Isfaran Zone would have played against the "perhaps" that stares us in the face in the emphatically mundane landscape of the Estonian Zone. An Isfaran Zone would have let us off the "perhaps" hook. From what we actually see of the Zone in the film, it could lie on the outskirts of many cities, of any northern city. It has nothing romantic or "fierce" to recommend it. Stanley

---

6. Bird, *Andrei Tarkovsky*, 149.

7. Grace Jantzen rightly warns "privileged western academics" off romanticizing the desert (Jantzen, "Touching [in] the Desert," 377).

Cavell recognizes a symbiotic relationship between fantasy and reality in cinema:

> It is a poor idea of fantasy which takes it to be a world apart from reality, a world clearly showing its unreality. Fantasy is precisely what reality can be confused with. It is through fantasy that our conviction of the worth of reality is established; to forgo our fantasies would be to forgo our touch with the world.[8]

Cavell's claim that confusion is an essential element in our relationship with fantasy returns us to Brocéliande, and to Oz, and to Bevans who recognizes that sometimes "what we are trying to understand will defy understanding."[9] In his "49 Asides for a Tragic Theatre," a manifesto originally published in the *Guardian* newspaper, the British playwright Howard Barker argued that

> the theatre must start to take its audience seriously. It must stop telling them stories they can understand.[10]

If the border between fantasy and reality were to be too clearly demarcated and policed—Cavell, Bevans, and Barker seem to suggest—this essential element of confusion, of failure to understand, to grasp, would be lost, and we would mistakenly take ourselves to be sure of where we stood. It is the job of science fiction, of fantasy, of tragic theater to show that where we stand may not be where we think we stand, that struggle and fallibility is part and parcel of the process. It is also the job of the gospels:

---

8. Cavell, *World Viewed*, 85.
9. Bevans, *Models of Contextual Theology*, 105.
10. Barker, "49 Asides," 655.

The Kingdom of God

> Being asked by the Pharisees when the kingdom of God would come, [Jesus] answered them, "The kingdom of God is not coming with signs to be observed, nor will they say, 'Look, here it is!' or 'There!' for behold, the kingdom of God is in the midst of you."[11]

Reality is revealed to be not as we first suspected. The limits and borders which we carefully police and patrol are arbitrary constructions that do not correspond to the actual limit situations which criss-cross our lives. And they certainly do not correspond to the way the limitless, the borderless transcends yet pervades reality: "we hold the divine nature to be unlimited and infinite."[12]

Cavell claims that fantasy is, as it were, a function of our coming to terms with reality. It is through the "as it were" that we reach the "as it is." This instrumental analysis of the role of fantasy conjures the plays of Shakespeare, where a magical forest or island serves the purpose of resettling the characters in reality. Or, it returns us to Brocéliande, where the fantasy is a quest-condition of a knight's becoming a real knight, or to Oz where Dorothy must confront and defeat analogues of her real demons. These fantasies are functional, and they function not by denying the surface phenomena, but by confusing them, problematizing them.

The final scenes of *Stalker*, once the men have returned from the Zone, reveal a landscape that appears to be continuous with the Zone. There is no "Here it is!" or "There!" Fantasy and reality, here and there are confused. Which is which? The Zone itself is absurd in its failure to live up to Professor Wallace's pronouncement; and the border is a farce—not because three middle-aged incompetents are able to cross it illegally on a motorized trolley cart

---

11. Luke 17:20–21.
12. Gregory of Nyssa, *Life of Moses* 1.7.

Perfect in Weakness

(what could sound more like a joke?)—but because it seems arbitrary and pointless. Crossing the border into the Zone, as we have seen, is hazardous and requires patience, experience, ingenuity, and daring. Crossing out of the Zone, this quarantined region that may be infected, that may have been visited by "inhabitants from the cosmic abyss," is apparently all too easy. Tarkovsky does not bother to depict the men's return journey at all. We cut, and they are all back in the bar where they first met, with a dog they met in the Zone. The proverbial shaggy dog perhaps?

The very pointlessness of the border, its arbitrary nature, causes us to rethink or call into question the neat and tidy schema we have learned to bring with us into the cinema. Our expectations and preconceptions relating to genre, narrative, plotting, and character are all destabilized by the experience of *Stalker*. The *stabilitas* which the film's billing as science-fiction and its skeletal narrative implies is denied. We are left with no authorial surety, no genre conventions, no character development to speak of. The plot just fizzles out in the general pointlessness.

Stability, Tarkovsky is saying, lies within the monastery walls, within our expectations, within culturally mandated norms and definitions. Stability belongs to the safe center. *Stalker* is shifting and shifty; it is errant. And it is concerned not with the center, but with the margins. Margins are dangerous, fluctuating, forgotten contexts. But they are also inseparable from our subjective experience of reality; we would not recognize the center as center were there no margins, just as we would not recognize reality without fantasy, sense without nonsense, wakefulness without dreaming.

Calling us to recognize and inhabit the margins is the voice of the prophet. Prophecy is heard primarily in apocalyptic. So, as Nariman Skakov rightly notes, the Zone

The Kingdom of God

in *Stalker* is an apocalyptic space.[13] I want to focus in the remainder of this chapter on this notion of apocalypse from four different critical standpoints.

APOCALYPSE AS DISASTER

In the non-technical sense of "apocalypse," the Zone appears to be a region of disaster, perhaps an environmental or industrial one.

> Science fiction films are not about science. They are about disaster, which is one of the oldest subjects of art.[14]

Again, the word "disaster" alerts us to Tarkovsky's experience in the early months of shooting *Stalker*, and to the effect of *délire* engulfing the reader in disaster. The manifest effects of disaster in the Zone can be accounted for, we are told, by the abandonment of the region after the suspected visit by aliens. The area has been evacuated by humans and reclaimed by nature, particularly by water. Pipes, tanks, and culverts all seem to have burst or broken. We have already acknowledged the baptismal significance of the water in *Stalker*. But I think it also represents release, a freeing following the "disaster." In one of the crystalline sequences at the center of the film, water is the medium through which, or by means of which, we observe bullets, syringes, coins, icons, guns, mirrors, and calendars lying at the bottom of a shallow tiled pool. And as we watch these drifting images through the water, we hear the gently flowing words of the Wife as she voices a passage from the book of Revelation, from the Apocalypse itself.[15] As Nariman Skakov notes,

13. Skakov, *Cinema of Tarkovsky*, 141–42, 149–53.
14. Sontag, "Imagination of Disaster," 213.
15. Rev 6:12–17.

61

however, the Wife's delivery of the text breaks down. "Her narration becomes unstable; she takes long pauses, and finally bursts into a neurotic giggle."[16] What has been lost in the water is the meaning both of the apparently miscellaneous, unrelated objects in the water and of the text we are hearing. Meaning itself is washed away, lost in the flow, in the "disaster," but somehow at the same time given a new sacramental import.

> *Délire* is first characterized by logorrhea, an unceasing flow of words, indication that communication is no longer possible.[17]

So, the Zone appears to be the result of an apocalypse that results in a disastrous loss of meaning, but which we also recognize somehow as home, as answer, as goal.

In fact, or rather in terms of the film's plot, the real apocalypse in *Stalker* is averted: at the last minute, the Professor forswears his intention to blow up the Room with a nuclear device he has secretly smuggled across the border. The Professor's destructive plans are impermissible; there is, as we have said, something sacralized about the Zone; human actions are curtailed, or somehow conditional on the Zone's will. Apocalypse postponed. Yet it hangs in the air like fallout, as possibility, as perhaps.

The endlessly running water in the film—as well as suggesting *délire*, babble, fluidity of meaning and of geography—might also indicate thaw. In the late 1970s, under Brezhnev (1906–82), the Soviet Union's dealings with the West were tense and troubling; what was effectively a proxy war between the superpowers broke out in Afghanistan in 1979, but relations were arguably no longer actually icy. Still, the prospect of nuclear armageddon and a subsequent

16. Skakov, *Cinema of Tarkovsky*, 151.
17. Lecercle, *Philosophy through the Looking-Glass*, 107.

post-Holocaust societal collapse continued to haunt the global imagination. In the United Kingdom, public information films advised householders on what to do in case of a nuclear attack, and how to avoid fallout.

The Zone is familiar, therefore, to generations brought up in an environment where apocalypse is permanently postponed, yet constantly predicted. It is in ruins, uninhabited, polluted, and it pollutes: the Stalker's daughter is disabled by a birth defect caused, we are told, by proximity to the Zone. Released seven years before the Chernobyl disaster, *Stalker* has sometimes been seen as prophetic (in the popular, "telling the future" sense) in its depiction of nuclear accident. The landscape is hostile, rebarbative, unbeautiful; like the thirty kilometer exclusion zone around the Chernobyl plant, it is abandoned and crumbling. Despite the references to meteorites and aliens, this looks like an apocalyptic place of our making.

"Apocalypse" in its biblical sense refers to a literary, prophetic genre: it is the poetics of waiting, of longing—for redemption, for freedom, for a Christ. In its more modern sense, "apocalypse" is the opposite; it is always after the event. It is understood no longer as waiting for the cause of our renewal, but living now with the effects of our own failure to renew ourselves or our world. Where apocalyptic literature in the Bible is an expression of hope, of faith, modern apocalyptic is always hope-less, faith-less. A disaster has befallen the word itself: the meaning of "apocalypse," as in a joke, as in *délire*, has been reversed. Biblical apocalyptic looks forward; in modern apocalyptic, there is no future to look forward to. We have lost faith.

Perfect in Weakness

APOCALYPSE AS REVELATION, AND AS JOKE

But the Zone is also a place of revelation, the literal meaning of "apocalypse." The Zone itself is supposed to be revelatory; it is billed as the locus of disclosure, of an unveiling. The question we immediately ask is, revelatory of what? This is the narrative hook of the film: what will happen in the Zone? What will be revealed? But from the start, Tarkovsky is asking a different question: revelatory to whom? When ultimately nothing happens, nothing is revealed, we are returned to ourselves as subjects:

> Revelation is only revelation when men and women are actually attending to the fact that God is always pouring love into our hearts by the Holy Spirit . . . Revelation is something that happens when a person opens himself or herself to reality.[18]

What I have called the "narrative hook" of *Stalker*, its skeletal plot, is all but unnecessary. Tarkovsky is not interested in "the logic of traditional drama," preferring to leave the spectator to attend to what is immediately presented on the screen,

> to become a participant in the process of discovering life, unsupported by ready-made deductions from the plot or ineluctable pointers by the author. He has at his disposal only what helps to penetrate to the deeper meaning of the complex phenomena represented in front of him.[19]

In other words, Tarkovsky's art and Bevans's transcendental model are perfectly in tune with one another; both place the attending subject at the center of their approach.

18. Bevans, *Models of Contextual Theology*, 105.
19. Tarkovsky, *Sculpting in Time*, 20.

For them both, it is the *process* of revelation that counts. Again, the difference between manifestation and practice.

By deploying the camera in idiosyncratic ways throughout the film, by repeatedly drawing our attention to eyes, and to the act of seeing, Tarkovsky makes this process of disclosure, of revelation explicit. By consistently placing the camera behind the heads of his characters, Tarkovsky asks us to share their perception of the Zone; we are the subjects of this experience. The visual grammar of *Stalker* is literally apocalyptic, revelatory.

Like apocalyptic, a joke functions through revelation. A punchline just is—a revelation. The ludicrous or bizarre elements in a joke make sense only retrospectively, with the revelation of the punchline. But there is very little—nothing even—that is ludicrous or bizarre about what we see in the Zone. Just ruined buildings, tunnels, rusting tanks, and sheds. All entirely ordinary. At one point, the Stalker leads his two companions down what is called the "Dry Tunnel"; it turns out to be anything but dry, a gushing conduit. The Stalker explains this away, as a joke.

So, what we are presented with is an environment, a landscape that appears flatly unhaunted, and ordinary. It is only the Stalker's claims in respect of the Zone that are ludicrous or bizarre. So again, what, if anything, is being revealed? Perhaps we might begin to look for an answer back in the Renaissance context of *serio ludere*, but transposed this time from philosophy and natural science to drama.

In 1957, the Canadian literary critic and theorist Northrop Frye published his seminal *The Anatomy of Criticism* in which he defines what he calls the "drama of the green world" in Shakespeare's comedies. What Frye identifies is a pattern: "a ritual theme of the triumph of life and love over the wasteland."

Perfect in Weakness

> The action of the comedy begins in a world represented as the normal world, moves into the green world, goes into metamorphosis there in which the comic resolution is achieved, and returns to the normal world.[20]

Plays which conform to this pattern include *The Two Gentlemen of Verona*, *A Midsummer Night's Dream*, *As You Like It*, and *The Merry Wives of Windsor*. The pattern of these comic plays, Frye suggests, is derived from earlier models available to Shakespeare and familiar to his audience: seasonal ritual-plays of medieval tradition in which the pastoral setting is a place of comic reversal and discovery; echoes here of Brocéliande and the landscapes of courtly, magical romance literature, as well as the *serio ludere* tropes of Cusanus and Bocchi. It is a region of experimentation and testing and trial. The characters who enter the "green world" will be returned to the real world transformed. So, while the characters in the play may be baffled, bemused by the ludic events and reverses of the "green world," we—the audience, safe in our objective world—are assured of their reality, and the ultimately benign direction of the plot. We are in on the joke.

By contrast, *Stalker*, while making the promise of its solidly sci-fi genre credentials—inhabitants of the cosmic abyss, meteorites, magic, and so on—fails to deliver on those promises. The characters' journey through the Zone feels like a children's game, a fool's fantasy. There are no special effects, no lights to see through the window, or alien artefacts lying helpfully around to assure us of the veracity of the Stalker's story. As far as the Writer and the Professor—and ourselves—are concerned, this green world could all be a delusion or a hoax, a money-making scam. The joke is on us.

20. Frye, *Anatomy of Criticism*, 182.

The Kingdom of God

Is the Stalker a John the Baptist figure, as we suggested earlier (the Baptist being another dangerous crosser of borders and denizen of the marginal zones)? Or is he a con artist who has fallen for his own con? Most pressing of all, how are we to tell the difference? In his analysis of *Stalker*, Robert Bird suggests

> it is difficult to rid oneself of the suspicion that [the Stalker] is actually leading the Writer, so to speak, up the garden path. The Stalker's strictures are improvised, not to protect his visitors from unknown dangers, but solely to stamp his authority on their quest.[21]

What Bird misses here of course, is the Stalker's own conviction, his faith. At no point is the character of the Stalker concerned with his own authority; only the authority of the Zone. To "lead someone up the garden path" is deliberately to mis-lead. Perhaps Bird's use of the expression is not idiomatic, but literal; after all, the Stalker leads the Writer and Professor through the tangled, overgrown garden of the Zone. Either way, the Stalker does not set out to deceive or to stamp his authority on anything; he risks everything on account of his belief in the power of the Room. Bird's use of the garden imagery, and our own (admittedly playful) attempt to save Bird's point by considering the possibility that the use of "garden path" is merely a reference to the natural setting of *Stalker*, calls to mind John Wisdom's famous paper "Gods," originally published in the journal of the *Proceedings of the Aristotelian Society* but reprinted in John Wisdom's *Philosophy and Psycho-analysis*. In that paper, Wisdom describes two men coming across a garden. One of the men suggests the garden is tended by a gardener, while the other believes it to be wild. Both parties are able

21. Bird, *Andrei Tarkovsky*, 163.

to claim support for their beliefs by reference to evidence already before them; no new evidence is forthcoming. Wisdom wants to make the point that the arguments of both men are rational, and are concerned with stating verifiable facts about the garden.

> The disputants speak as if they are concerned with a matter of scientific fact, or of trans-sensual, trans-scientific and metaphysical fact, but still of fact and still a matter about which reasons for and against may be offered.[22]

Neither of these men is "leading the other up the garden path." Both men argue in good faith, and both are seeing and experiencing the garden in radically different ways. Tarkovsky's Zone is Wisdom's garden brought to dramatic life. We are no longer in Shakespeare's "green world," or in Oz; Tarkovsky's camera remains coolly observant, offering no clues as to how to interpret the Stalker's claims in respect of the Zone.

And in this respect, *Stalker* is less like Shakespeare, or L. Frank Baum, and more reminiscent, perhaps unexpectedly, of Jane Austen. In *Northanger Abbey*, the heroine, Catherine Morland, is morbidly obsessed with gothic fiction, as Quixote is obsessed with tales of knightly derring-do, and she cannot help seeing perfectly innocent occurrences and objects in the real world as clues, as evidence of a nefarious and dastardly plot going on around her. Happenstance becomes significance. For her, a locked trunk, the wind gusting in the chimney, billowing curtains, all conform to expectations, to a conventional schema which she imaginatively maps onto her experience of the world. But the old manuscript she finds hidden in a cabinet turns out to be a laundry list. A mysteriously locked room, when finally

22. Wisdom, "Gods," 156.

entered, turns out to be a perfectly normal and respectable apartment. Catherine's suspicions as to the death of Henry Tilney's mother cause Henry to take her to task:

> Consult your own understanding, your own sense of the probable, your own observation of what is passing around you.[23]

Tilney's rational, empirical, enlightened (and patronizing) advice could perhaps have been wisely taken by those entering the Zone. What grounds do the Writer and Professor have to believe that what they are being told is true? None whatsoever beyond rumour and the reports of the Stalker himself, the authority of a man entirely without authority. Catherine's experience of what is going on around her in the novel is paradoxical. It is not hers inasmuch as it is not empirically warranted, unverified by cool reason, and therefore unreal, and yet it is radically hers in that it is a product of her own subjective imagination. Catherine Morland and the Stalker, while they may not be misleading, may well be mistaken; we have no good hermeneutical grounds to trust either of them. In contrast to Catherine or the Stalker, the Writer and the Professor would seem—like Tilney—to be trustworthy. They are both worldly, successful men. (Like the aristocrats in Shakespeare's comedies who find themselves brought low in the forest.) The Stalker, on the other hand, lives hand to mouth: his life is hard, dangerous, and poor. But he is faithful.

APOCALYPSE AS PROPHECY

"Apocalypse" is, of course, a religious-literary term. And *Stalker* is rich in religious—and particularly apocalyptic—imagery and allusion, but it is always ambiguous, open to

23. Austen, *Northanger Abbey*, 159.

interpretation. So, when we encounter a devotional image of John the Baptist from Van Eyck's Ghent altarpiece, it has been discarded, submerged—appropriately—under the water; the Stalker is laughed at and mocked for being God's fool; the crown of thorns is placed on the least Christlike head in the story, the Writer's; we hear a distorted, redacted version of the Emmaus story from Luke's gospel, and also passages read by the Wife from the book of Revelation. The image of the well in the film calls to mind John 4:1–15.

And when the Stalker, the Writer, and the Professor first arrive in the Zone, a number of electricity poles lean precariously this way and that, silhouetted against a flat grey sky, forming a sort of muddled calvary scene. This is clearly a religious image. But it is doing more than simply adverting to a general theme of the film, and it deserves close attention. Firstly, of course, these crosses are empty. Are they waiting for their victims? In which case, are we to assume these three men are walking toward their crosses, their deaths? If so, which of them is Christ? To assume that the Stalker plays this role would be premature; after all, it is the Writer who puts on the crown of thorns, and it is the Professor who breaks and shares the bread (in the form of his sandwiches.)

But perhaps the crosses are empty because the bodies have already been taken down. The general state of dilapidation in the Zone suggests that we have arrived after the apocalyptic event. The electricity pole crosses are therefore haunting reminders of a *deus absconditus*. We are too late.

I have already said that apocalyptic literature in the Bible is the absurdly, unjustifiably faithful and hopeful expression of an oppressed people for a new dawn, a new future.

> The kingship and dominion
> and the greatness of the kingdoms

The Kingdom of God

under the whole heaven
shall be given to the people of the
holy ones of the Most High.[24]

It singles out the oppressed as the chosen or elected who are ultimately to be delivered into glory at the eschaton.

> And this good news of the kingdom will be proclaimed throughout the world, as a testimony to the nations; and then the end will come.[25]

At the heart of all apocalyptic writing, therefore, is a dual movement—into the wilderness, the proving ground, in order to return, by way of deliverance into that which has been promised at the end.

> Then they shall know that I am the Lord their God because I sent them into exile among the nations, and then gathered them into their own land. I will leave none of them behind; and I will never again hide my face from them, when I pour out my spirit on the house of Israel.[26]

In essence, apocalyptic presents in narrative form what the Neoplatonist thinkers we have already encountered analyzed as procession and return, which finds cosmic Christian expression in the fall and the resurrection, in the first man's expulsion from Eden, and then in the Son of Man, at the atonement, opening the gates of paradise to the righteous.

In Luke's Gospel, this notion of apocalyptic is encapsulated in the story of the criminals crucified alongside Jesus.[27] While one criminal mockingly tells Jesus to save

24. Deut 7:27.
25. Matt 24:14.
26. Ezek 39:28–29.
27. Luke 23:32–43.

himself, and to save him too while he is at it, the other criminal acknowledges that they have been rightly condemned, but that Jesus is innocent. He asks his fellow criminal, "Do you not fear God?"[28] This fear is the stamp, the imprimatur of apocalyptic; it is the prerequisite: "Fear of the Lord is the beginning of wisdom."[29] Fear is the rupture through which the kingdom of God can first be revealed. The Stalker in Tarkovsky's film is, above all, fearful. He is not driven by necessity, or curiosity; one suspects he is not driven by hope, but by fear.

Jesus tells the fearful criminal, "Truly I tell you, this day you will be with me in Paradise."[30] The place of ultimate glory is promised from the place of ultimate debasement: these are the poles of the ultimate journey. What appears to be shared, concrete, mundane experience is revealed to be otherwise by a righteous, fearful (and absurd) recognition of an underlying apocalyptic truth. It is, as Collicutt suggested, simply a question of turning. "I must turn aside and look at this great sight."[31]

For Tarkovsky, shooting *Stalker* in 1977, just as Brezhnev's politburo enacted the draconian Seventh Soviet Constitution, this prophetic reading of "apocalyptic" in *Stalker* could be interpreted as risky critique of an increasingly corrupt and suspicious regime drifting back into the habits and horrors of Josef Stalin's dictatorship. So, we see rusting military and industrial hardware, the lethal but inept border guards; the rules and regulations that the Stalker transgresses could all appear to invoke political authoritarianism. Above all, the Room itself—a wish endlessly offered, endlessly withheld—sounds like a satire on the empty promises/

28. Luke 23:40.
29. Prov 9:10; Pss 111:10; 33:8.
30. Luke 23:43.
31. Exod 3:3.

propaganda of the politburo. But there is little or no evidence in Tarkovsky's diaries or in his other writings that *Stalker* was ever intended to deliver a political (let alone an anti-Soviet) message. Nonetheless, I do think there is a sociopolitical way of reading the apocalyptic in *Stalker*.

The Zone is bracketed from mundane reality. It is marginalized and proves not to be assimilable into the rest of the world. It is the radically other. In this respect, its status—in the world, but not of the world—is akin to that of both the artist, and the prophet. Its place is at the margins, on the outside, *extra*, beyond the city gates. Here is the territory of the artist and the prophet:

> Thus said the Lord to me: Go and stand in the People's Gate, by which the kings of Judah enter and by which they go out, and in all the gates of Jerusalem, and say to them: Hear the word of the Lord, you kings of Judah, and all Judah, and all the inhabitants of Jerusalem who enter by these gates.[32]

The activity of the artist, according to Bevans's transcendental model, "might be a better analogy for doing theology than that of the philosopher."[33] What the artist and the prophet share is a heard demand to cross the frontier, to go beyond: it is a dangerous journey, expressed in prophetic discourse and, I suggest, in the flights of *délire*; it is effected always and only by means of the imagination:

> The prophet engages in futuring fantasy. The prophet does not ask if the vision can be implemented, for questions of implementation are of no consequence until the vision can be imagined. The imagination must come before

32. Jer 17:19–20.
33. Bevans, *Models of Contextual Theology*, 107.

> the implementation. Our culture is competent to implement almost anything and to imagine almost nothing. The same royal consciousness that makes it possible to implement anything and everything is the one that shrinks imagination because imagination is a danger. Thus every totalitarian regime is frightened of the artist. It is the vocation of the prophet to keep alive the ministry of the imagination, to keep on conjuring and proposing futures alternative to the single one the king wants to urge as the only thinkable one.[34]

The danger inherent in the prophetic imagination alerts us again to all the ideas nested in "apocalypse": disaster, fear, revelation, the madness (*délire*) of the message which could get us locked up or put away. It is the danger we encounter at the frontier, at the border, the People's Gate. The banishment of the prophet to the margins, to the gates, would have resonated deeply with Tarkovsky who was certainly frightening to the totalitarian regime, and who will be forced to live the last four years of his life as an unhappy exile from the Soviet Union, spending long periods of time away from his beloved wife, and his son, Andrei Jr. (who was not allowed to leave the Soviet Union). The Zone becomes an analogue for exile, the imaginative standpoint of the artist, the prophet, the watcher. The one who holds faith.

APOCALYPSE AS CINEMA

Kaluptein in Greek literally means to veil, to screen off. In the cinema, we are presented with the world without being present to the world; this apparently magical opportunity

---

34. Brueggemann, *Prophetic Imagination*, 40.

The Kingdom of God

is made possible by means of a screen, a veil. For Žižek, "the Zone is the place onto which you can project your beliefs . . . [it is] ultimately the very whiteness of the screen."[35] The whiteness of the screen may be the limit situation of cinema, but phenomenologically speaking, it is invisible of course. The screen is paradoxically a veil that exposes, a curtain that claims to be a window, unbreachable yet breached (apparently) by light merely. The screen is transfigured.

> And [Jesus] was transfigured before them, and his clothes became dazzling white, such as no one on earth could bleach them.[36]

The transfigured Jesus becomes the white screen by means of which a new reality is revealed. Likewise, the screen is a necessary condition for revelation, for apocalypse. The ultimate model for cinema is Christ himself.

Yet cinema is also apocalyptic in an unexpected and apparently unhelpful way. It reveals—all too manifestly—the skeptic's grounds for skepticism: that our experience of a continuous phenomenal flow of reality is open to radical doubt. In Flann O'Brien's comic but uncanny novel *The Third Policeman*, the fictional philosopher de Selby is led to assert, somewhat Eleatically, that "a journey is an hallucination" because human existence is a succession of static experiences each infinitely brief,

> a conception which he is thought to have arrived at from examining some old cinematograph films.[37]

Cinema is thus a conundrum, an illusion that appears to reveal the truth that reality is itself an illusion.

---

35. Fiennes, *Pervert's Guide to the Cinema*.
36. Mark 9:2–3.
37. O'Brien, *Third Policeman*, 52.

Perfect in Weakness

The persistence of vision, the name given to the fact that projecting twenty-four static frames per second is enough to trick de Selby's brain, all our brains, into believing that we are seeing a continuous flow of visual data, reveals our own epistemological fallibility, our own failure to see reality. Film is revelatory, therefore, of one thing: the true depth of our "perhaps predicament."[38] The border between fantasy and reality, the known and the unknown, the knowable and the unknowable turns out to be blurred, and pervasive, like yeast mixed through flour.[39] So here, finally is the deep paradigm for the Zone:

> And again he said, "To what shall I compare the Kingdom of God?"[40]

A kingdom that is like yeast sifted through flour, everywhere and yet imperceptible, or tiny—all but imperceptible—like a mustard seed,[41] hidden so as to be imperceptible, like buried treasure,[42] that will come unexpectedly, like a thief imperceptibly in the night.[43] It is difficult not to see the comic element in Jesus' parables of the kingdom. It is everywhere, staring us in the face, and yet we cannot perceive it, so beguiled are we by our own phenomenal experience.

---

38. "A little twitch in our optic nerve, a shock effect: twenty-four illuminated frames in a second, darkness in between, the optic nerve incapable of registering darkness. At the editing table, when I run the strip of film through, frame by frame, I still feel that dizzy sense of magic of my childhood: in the darkness of the wardrobe, I slowly wind one frame after another, see almost imperceptible changes, wind faster—a movement" (Bergman, *Magic Lantern*, 74–75).

39. Matt 13:33; Luke 13:21.

40. Luke 13:20.

41. Mark 4:31–32; Matt 13:31–32; Luke 13:18–19.

42. Matt 13:44.

43. 1 Thess 5:2.

THE KINGDOM OF GOD

The kingdom of God cannot be separable from the world; it is not here or there; it is among us.[44] The border between the Zone and the "real" world is a joke. And so—in the Zone, as in the "green world," or the kingdom of heaven—society is inverted: the first will be last, the criminal becomes the guide; the fool becomes the instructor; failure is the only route to success. The comedy lies, as in Shakespeare's "green world," in the reversal of our expectations, in an overturning, a punchline which we know is coming but which, for now, remains imperceptible, out of sight.

Take the parable of the workers in the vineyard.[45] Those who work a full day are paid the same as those who show up for only an hour's work. Or, look at the rejoicing of the father at the return of his wayward, spendthrift son who, by rights, ought to be punished or rejected rather than welcomed with open arms.[46] And the wedding banquet—when the guests fail to attend, the master of the house orders people off the street to join him.[47] These are all comic reversals.

> The wolf shall live with the lamb,
>   the leopard shall lie down with the kid,
> the calf and the lion and the fatling together,
>   and a little child shall lead them.
> The cow and the bear shall graze,
>   their young shall lie down together;
>   and the lion shall eat straw like the ox.
> The nursing child shall play over the hole of the asp,
>   and the weaned child shall put its hand on the adder's den.
> They will not hurt or destroy
>   on all my holy mountain;

---

44. Luke 17:21.
45. Matt 20:1–16.
46. Luke 15:11–32.
47. Luke 14:15–24; Matt 22:1–10.

for the earth will be full of the knowledge of the Lord
as the waters cover the sea.[48]

Here is the ultimate, ludic, topsy-turvy *délire* description of the peaceful kingdom of God. These are places—the Zone, Oz, the "green world," the kingdom—reserved for the absurd, the impossible. This is a realm where contextual norms are overturned, Saturnalia-style, where "perhaps" prevails, where Tilney's patronizing advice to Catherine will not apply. So, the question is, how are we to navigate this Zone? How are we to reach the Room, the punchline, when all will be revealed? This kingdom, the paradise that Jesus promises from the cross, the claims for the Zone made by the Stalker, are available to us, only through faith.

CINEMA AS ICON

Before the three men set off for the Zone, they *rendezvous* in the bar by the docks. We have seen this down-at-heel bar before, in the title sequence, when we watched the lugubrious patron opening up. With its flickering fluorescent tube, grubby glass-fronted door, and wet tiled floor, it has the stripped down, (dys)functional air of an establishment frequented only by the hardest of hardened drinkers.

By assembling the three men around one of the bar's few tables, Tarkovsky appears to tantalize us with one of the most subtle and penetrating visual references in *Stalker*. The arrangement of the three figures around the table, the empty space perhaps waiting for a fourth facing toward us as the camera slowly closes on the group, calls to mind (and seems *designed* to call to mind) one of the most famous

---

48. Isa 11:6–9. Perhaps Hynek would dismiss this vision too as a string of "worthy platitudes" akin to "be good, stop fighting, live in love and brotherhood," and so on.

THE KINGDOM OF GOD

images of orthodoxy: Andrei Rublev's icon, the *Hospitality of Abraham*.[49] Rublev's icon is generally read as a representation of the Holy Trinity. A number of arguments have been made as to which figure represents which Person. It is also suggested—somewhat fancifully to my mind—that Rublev conceived the icon as incorporating a mirror in which the viewer's gazing face would be reflected, allowing the worshipper to be drawn into, and included in the relationship of, the Trinity. With or without the mirror mechanism, Rublev's icon is clearly designed to invite the viewer into the space of the image: there is a place at the table for you. Rather than the aggressively pointing finger of World War I recruiting posters, the icon offers an open hand, a gesture of welcome. It is its profound, pervading sense of welcome that has secured this particular icon's centrality in any discussion of Orthodox art and spirituality.

So, what on earth does Tarkovsky intend by transposing Rublev's sublime meditation on the Holy Trinity into a seedy, dockside bar, replacing the Persons of the Trinity with a drunk writer, a disaffected scientist, and a criminal trafficker? I do not think we can settle for the obvious (and obviously trite) sermonizing claim that Tarkovsky wants us to the see the Trinity at work, living and present even here; nowhere is God-forsaken.

In situations like this, where the film's imagery seems to suggest a hidden meaning, we need to be especially cautious, taking care not to fall into the trap we identified in the introduction to this book of drawing out meaning from the film, of decoding the film's underlying message. Note how even our language suggests a certain sort of disclosure: we draw meaning *out* from inside; the message of the film lies *under*, below the film's surface. But there is no under the

49. I am indebted to Elijah Davidson for drawing my attention to this parallel.

surface; there is no inside. Film is absolutely superficial. The sort of apocalypse or unveiling we have been discussing in the previous sections of this chapter is of an entirely different sort: it reveals itself only as surface.

Cinema, as we have already noted, is an illusion of time (persistence); it is also an illusion of space (perspective.) It is not that images appear to move; it is that they appear to move in three-dimensional space. The train pulling into the station is going to plough through the nickelodeon itself. It is coming toward us. But there is no toward, only our perspective. How quickly and completely we have come to associate our point of view with the camera! We yearn to be the camera. The root of cinema is this experience of a subjectivity not our own, but which we feel to be radically *ours*. What allows for this bewitching blend of persistence and perspective is the screen, the screen's capacity, its receptivity. It readily receives us as camera, as point of view. And it is in this respect that cinema most resembles iconography.

Like the surface of an icon, the screen's receptivity is a function of its flatness, its unperceivable yet permanent blankness. As we have already noted, to look for an *underlying* message in cinema is to look in precisely the wrong place. Lying behind the screen is nothing, or worse than nothing: the nightmarish running of the same film, but back to front.

Many icons are designed to sit in a complex frame, the iconostasis, an architectural structure in an Orthodox church that divides the nave from the sanctuary. It is a semipermeable membrane, penetrable only by priests allowed into the sanctuary where the sacramental mysteries are performed. This combination of architectural position and liturgical function has given rise to icons popularly being described as windows to heaven.[50] They offer views

50. So, in her recent book *Walking on Water: Reflections on Faith*

The Kingdom of God

out of this world, and *into* the kingdom of God.[51] Or so the theory goes. While I would not want to dispute the beauty of this idea, I think there may be another way to consider both icons and cinema screens.

Rublev and Tarkovsky, with the *Hospitality of Abraham* and *Stalker* respectively, seem to offer a different view. Rather than seeing *through* the icon or the screen to another world, a zone, or a kingdom to come, they encourage us to consider the surface. Both Tarkovsky and Rublev suggest that it is at the surface where the magical blending of subjectivities takes place through the marriage of persistence and perspective. Here, there is something genuinely Trinitarian at play. Rather than the simple, linear relationship suggested by the notion of a transparent window, we find the complex triangularity of a reflective surface, or a surface that offers the possibility of reflecting back to us an image of ourselves transformed, converted, freed.[52] Or if this is a window, it is Roy Neary's window, nulling our

---

and Art, Madeleine L'Engle defines an icon as "an open window through which we can be given a new glimpse of the love of God" (L'Engle, *Walking on Water*, 19).

51. Icons "are themselves fundamentally religious, of the other world rather than of this" (Talbot Rice, *Byzantine Art*, 150). Talbot Rice also claims that an icon's "significance lies below the surface" (*Byzantine Art*, 150). I am arguing precisely the opposite: the icon's significance is readable off of the surface.

52. This is the contemplative insight of St. Clare of Assisi, founder of the Franciscan Order of the Poor Clares in 1212. In a letter to Agnes of Prague, Clare writes, "Place your mind in the mirror of eternity! Place your soul in the brilliance of glory! Place your heart in the figure of the divine substance! And transform your whole being into the image of the Godhead itself through contemplation" (Clare of Assisi's "Third Letter to Agnes of Prague" in *Francis and Clare: The Complete Works*, 200). Mirror, brilliant light, image, contemplations, transformation; this is an instruction manual for the building of a cinema of the soul, Tarkovsky's cinema.

neighbors, their cars, their baseball games. It tells us more about ourselves than anything beyond or outside. There is nothing beyond, nothing outside.

I am forcefully reminded here of how upset I was as a child watching the final scene in Gerry and Sylvia Anderson's brilliantly conceived, if not brilliantly executed, *Journey to the Far Side of the Sun* (1969). In that final scene, the retired director of an international space program (played by Patrick Wymark), now in a wheelchair and suffering from dementia, catches sight of his reflection in a mirror at the end of a corridor. He suddenly believes he can escape *through* the mirror from this mirror-Earth in which he feels trapped, where he knows he does not belong, where he is living a sort of Heideggerian nightmare, perpetually forced to call his own being here into question. Paradoxically, the mirror offers escape *from* reversal. A modern Narcissus, he wheels himself desperately toward the mirror's surface, its limit, his own limit, his reflection. He crashes through the mirror and dies.[53] I cannot honestly pretend to have lined all this up as a child! But the existential tragedy of the scene was deeply felt nonetheless, and has remained with me ever since.

Immediately before the scene in the bar in *Stalker* when the three men gather for the first time, the Writer has been outside, on the docks, talking to a girl in a fur coat. It is clearly the morning after a night before. And, still drunk, he is pontificating on the dullness of the world. "There is no such thing as telepathy, ghosts, or flying saucers."[54] He continues:

> Iron laws govern the world, which makes it unbearably dull. And these laws, alas, are inviolable.

---

53. Parrish, *Journey to the Far Side of the Sun*.
54. Tarkovsky, *Andrei Tarkovsky: Collected Screenplays*, 382.

The Kingdom of God

> Don't count on flying saucers, that would be just too interesting.[55]

Giving a hint, perhaps, as to how we are to interpret the imagery of the following "Rublev" scene in the bar, the Writer goes on to compare God to a triangle. In the Writer's view, the triangle is a symbol of monotonous, mathematical regularity, of law.

> There is a triangle abc, which is similar to xyz. Can't you feel the depressing tedium that such a statement contains?[56]

In *Stalker*, Tarkovsky offers an emphatic, profound, and numinous "no" to the Writer's question. The unplumbable holy mystery of "there is a triangle abc, which is similar to xyz" is the twisted trinitarian truth attested to in *Stalker*, and which is revealed only through faith.

---

55. Tarkovsky, *Andrei Tarkovsky: Collected Screenplays*, 382.
56. Tarkovsky, *Andrei Tarkovsky: Collected Screenplays*, 382.

4

FAITH

We do not see our emblems;
there is no longer any prophet,
and there is no one among us who knows how long.

—Ps 74:9

If at first you don't succeed, failure may be your style.

—Quentin Crisp

Whether or not the Zone really is the site of a close encounter with something alien or simply a figment of a warped imagination, the Stalker's faith in it is the key to the film. It is the glue that holds this desperate man, this joke-plot, together. He has gambled his marriage and staked his life on the impossible, the unprovable, the absurd. He is the dramatic realization of what Kierkegaard calls the knight of faith:

Faith

> On this the knight of faith is clear: all that can save him is the absurd; and this he grasps by faith.[1]

While Kierkegaard's knight of faith is a towering figure, an Abraham, a hero of almost superhuman stature, Tarkovsky's Stalker is like Quixote, like a child. Less Abraham, more Isaac. Faith for the Stalker is not what Dag Hammarskjöld damned as "metaphysical magic" reserved for a "spiritual elite."[2] It is not a source of power or strength. Faith does not make the journey possible; this is a journey through the impossible. Faith does not make the journey easier; trial—as for Chrétien's knight of the Round Table, so for Kierkegaard's knight of faith—is of this journey's essence. Faith does not reveal the journey's goal; ultimately the goal is unattainable. Faith is folly, literally the act of a fool. *Stalker* is an extended, heartfelt hymn to naïveté.

In an extraordinary, almost hallucinatory sequence in the middle of the film, the Stalker relates a story to the Writer and Professor. He describes two men on a journey who are conversing when a third man joins them on the road. But they are prevented from recognizing him. "What are you discussing?" the man asks. "And why are you sad?" It is a verbatim quote from the Road to Emmaus story in Luke's Gospel in which the risen Christ appears to two of his disciples who do not recognize him.[3] It is, in essence, an alien visitation story, ticking all Hynek's boxes and including Bowie's augmentations: the message is for you; it separates you from society; it puts you at odds with the world, and is therefore dangerous. The story is about faith—a lack of it, finding it. The Emmaus story also clearly echoes the

---

1. Kierkegaard, *Fear and Trembling*, 75–76.
2. Hammarskjöld, *Markings*, 106.
3. Luke 24:13–18.

action of *Stalker*: three men on a journey. But the passage has deeper functional resonances. The Emmaus story, like *Stalker* as a whole, is at least partly about seeing, about revelation. It is also—again like *Stalker*—a joke, with a setup and a punchline. Although here, in this retelling, the Stalker withholds that punchline.

In Luke's Gospel, Christ discloses his identity to the disciples later when he breaks bread with them. Significantly, the Stalker cuts off the Emmaus story before this revelation; he leaves the story hanging with a question. He asks the Writer and the Professor: "Are you awake?" A question that obliquely refers perhaps to the inability of the disciples in the story to "wake up" to the reality in front of them. But in the context of the film narrative, it is a strange question to ask, coming as it does, immediately after a slow, back-and-forth tracking shot in which the Professor and then the Writer open their eyes to look almost directly into the camera. They are obviously awake; or are they?

Back in Shakespeare's "green world," Demetrius asks, toward the end of *A Midsummer Night's Dream*:

> Are you sure
> That we are awake? It seems to me
> That yet we sleep, we dream.[4]

The nature of wakefulness, our phenomenological reception of the physical world, and the epistemological status of the seen, in the "green world" and in the Zone, are open to question, to doubt, to perhaps. And are any of us in the cinema actually awake at this moment to the fact we are willfully submitting to an illusion? Again, we ought to be open to the possibility that the Stalker's question may be addressed to us sitting in the dark, watching light and shadows flickering on a screen, a cinematic simulacrum.

4. Shakespeare, *Midsummer Night's Dream*, 4.1.189.

Faith

Plato's cave dwellers are prisoners, tied down and forced to look straight ahead at the wall/screen.[5] We bought tickets! We chose this. Are you awake?

And the question's challenge goes deeper still. The Stalker describes the Zone to his two companions in the following way:

> Our moods, our thoughts, our emotions, our feelings can bring about change here. And we are in no condition to comprehend them . . . That's how the Zone is . . . In fact at any moment it is exactly as we devise it, in our consciousness.[6]

How are we to take this statement? Of course, it could simply be an expression of our first definition of "apocalypse": this ruination and spoliation is our fault, our responsibility, a mess of our own making. Or could it be Tarkovsky's own voice—the voice of the cinematic auteur—breaking in, alerting us to the fact that this landscape, this environment, this journey is exactly as he has devised it in his consciousness? Does it serve to remind us that this is not a real landscape at all, that it is created in a camera and projected on to a white screen (a screen that remains white and blank all the time, and to which we bring our moods, our thoughts, and emotions)? Or should we take it as directly addressing us, an exposé of our own subjectivity? The Zone is not delivered to our consciousness; we devise it, or dream it by an act of subjective imagination.

The use of the word "devising" is clearly meant to capture more than the idea of simply reading our own psychological or cultural constructs—like Catherine Morland—back onto a subsisting external reality; it is more than mapping our Quixotic, *Billy Liar* dreams onto what

5. *Resp.* 514a.

6. Tarkovsky, *Andrei Tarkovsky: Collected Screenplays*, 395.

is actually there. This is constructing "there" from scratch. *Stalker* plays with the possibility that subjective experience might somehow be inventive, literally creative. In other words, Bird was right (albeit by mistake) to accuse the Stalker of leading his charges "up the garden path." To "lead someone up the garden path" might actually be constitutive of reality.

And the Stalker's line concerning reality being exactly as we devise it in our consciousness returns us to Gregory of Nyssa, who categorically rejects the Stoic notion of knowledge as degrees of possession or "grasping." For Gregory, all knowledge is conjectural, improvisatory, knowledge-toward: *epinoia*. The object of thought always remains essentially unknown. *Epinoia* thus stands between knowledge and ignorance. Hans Urs von Balthasar describes Gregory's concept of *epinoia* in this way:

> The "Logos of creation," the essence of things, always escapes us. God alone knows it. Eunomius is like a child who would like to grab hold of a ray of the sun. He wants to understand rather than adore.[7]

The object—every object—remains essentially unknown and unknowable in the great mystery of the world, its participation in God. For Gregory, all human knowledge, therefore, is "true only to the degree it renounces by a perpetual effort its own nature, which is to 'seize' its prey."[8] We must hold as suspect Henry Tilney's call for understanding, observation, and reasoning, just as we ought to doubt Catherine's imaginative cultural borrowings. Tilney's epistemological approach, as much as Catherine's, is fallible, "inventive." *Epinoia* is "an inventive (εὑρετικὴ) approach to

7. Balthasar, *Presence and Thought*, 92–93.
8. Balthasar, *Presence and Thought*, 93.

the unknown."⁹ The verb from which εὑρετικὴ is derived can be translated "to find" or "to devise." True knowledge, Gregory seems to be suggesting, is not so much grasping as straining toward, as a process aimed at discovery, as devising. There is a recognition here that our knowledge is always and necessarily incomplete. We are forced to rely instead on faith.

> It is only the Christian attitude, that is to say, faith, that corresponds truly to the spiritual nature of God and to the revelatory character of all of creation. Faith is definitively the only knowledge that conforms to our condition (μόνον σύμμετρόν ἐστι τῇ ἡμετέρᾳ κατανοήσει), a faith that is something completely other than a "conviction", which would still be only a form of knowing.¹⁰

While creation is revelatory, it can never be fully revealed to us. We may be turned toward the light, but we are still sitting in the dark. The notion that reality is as we devise it or invent it, that all knowledge (if it counts as knowledge at all) is at least partly improvisatory and dependent on faith, brings to mind those familiar moments in cartoons when a character steps out from or dashes over the edge of a cliff—and continues running. The character continues to run until their being no longer supported by the ground comes to their consciousness; as though the force of gravity were conditional on our being conscious of

---

9. Gregory of Nyssa, *Contra Eunomium 12*, 2 (*PG* 45:969C).

10. Balthasar, *Presence and Thought*, 94–95. With respect: Balthasar's translation is a little loose here. I would argue that faith for Gregory is not knowledge, or any form of knowledge. We might render Gregory's words as: "faith (πίστιν) alone is the measure of our understanding" (Gregory of Nyssa, *Contra Eunomium 10* [*PG* 45: 832B]; Balthasar mistakenly gives this reference as 832D).

it, or that we could counteract it by choosing not to believe in it, or notice it.

> He said, "Come." So Peter got out of the boat, started walking on the water, and came towards Jesus. But when he noticed the strong wind he became frightened, and beginning to sink, he cried out, "Lord, save me!"[11]

Knowing, noticing, is Peter's downfall.

If this ability to faithfully devise reality according to our own will sounds like the power of a superhero, it is certainly not conceived in this way by Tarkovsky or Jesus. Since, as Gregory argues, it appears we have no direct, unimagined access to reality, we are thrown back on faith. Every step we take, we take on water. In other words, faith is the only interpretative, heuristic strategy available to us. This faith is not a source of strength; rather, it is a symptom or function of a necessary naïveté deriving from our epistemological fallibility. We can walk on water, we can throw mountains into the sea,[12] not because we have superpowers, but because we have no power at all, except our faithful imaginations which correspond to, or are constitutive of, a radically subjective reality. This powerlessness is illustrated by the Stalker in his quoting from the *Tao-Te-Ching*:

> When a man is just born he is weak and flexible. When he dies he is hard and insensitive. When a tree is growing, it is tender and pliant, but when it's dry and hard, it dies. Hardness and strength are death's companions. Pliancy and weakness are expressions of the freshness of being. Because of what has hardened we will never win.[13]

---

11. Matt 14:29–30.
12. Mark 11:23.
13. Tarkovsky, *Stalker*.

Faith

Immediately following this passage, the Stalker prays for his two companions in words that closely echo Saint Paul in 2 Corinthians 12:9: "for power is made perfect in weakness." The Stalker prays: "Let them be helpless like children. Because weakness is a great thing and strength is nothing."[14] The weakness the Stalker has in mind here, I suggest, is faith. Faith is our response to the "perhaps predicament." We are left floundering, as in a joke, epistemologically reliant only on our imaginations, our heuristical attempts to master the "perhaps," to translate the absurdity into something we can understand. But we cannot do this by grasping, by an act of our own understanding. Like characters in a joke, we are left "faithfully" waiting, wanting, collaborating in a fictive "game."

"Devising reality" suggests the philosophical territory explored by the most imaginative of the modern empiricists: Bishop Berkeley (1685–1753.) According to Berkeley (and also Gregory of Nyssa, interestingly), there is no underlying material substrate in which perceivable qualities inhere. For Berkeley, nothing material exists, and nothing exists independently of mind. What we perceive as physical reality is an agglomeration of received ideas (perceivable qualities) of sense.

> Take away the sensations of softness, moistness, redness, tartness, and you take away the cherry. Since it is not a being distinct from sensations; a cherry, I say, is nothing but a congeries of sensible impressions, or ideas perceived by various senses.[15]

Our perceptions (or "ideas"), Berkeley argued, are immaterial, so therefore we have no grounds to suppose that

---

14. Tarkovsky, *Stalker*.
15. Berkeley, *Three Dialogues*, 130.

the external world is itself anything but immaterial, made up only of ideas. He avoids the danger of solipsism by introducing God, the mind which sustains all ideas through a maximally powerful imagination.[16] So, for Berkeley, the guarantor of accuracy when it comes to our experience of reality is a benign, dependable, infallible God in whose mind the ideas of creation inhere.

Reframing Berkeleyan immaterialism in a context of fallibility and failure and doubt, *Stalker* poses a stark question: if the Zone is exactly as we devise it in our consciousness, where is the need for God? What role for the Room which, in terms of the film's narrative, proves impotent anyway? In the film, there appears to be no external guarantor; the final proof, in the form of the efficacy of the Room, is withheld, denied. We are, in other words, plunged into the solipsism that Berkeley was able to avoid, and the radical subjectivism that Bevans recognizes as a danger of the transcendental model: "What or who provides the criterion of subjective authenticity?"[17]

And this solipsism returns us to Tarkovsky's state of mind during the filming of *Stalker*. As we have already seen, he felt profoundly isolated, let down by his crew, by Mosfilm, his production company. And his frustrations find expression in the idea of the lonely, embattled artist, railing against a stable society that conspires against freedom. The psychological isolation of the director is translated into the existential isolation of the Stalker. The apparent solipsism of the lone creative artist/prophet becomes the literal solipsism of the human-god who creates or devises their own reality. It is hard not to see the Stalker as an analogue for Tarkovsky himself, an isolated figure struggling through a

16. Berkeley, *Three Dialogues*, 133.
17. Bevans, *Models of Contextual Theology*, 108.

Faith

landscape that is unbiddable, hostile, and yet who must create, who must bring an entire world into being.

Tellingly, this devising, this creative act does not entail authority or power over the created environment; as the Stalker says, the Zone is capricious; it can kill you. It may be our creation, but in creating it we relinquish control. This is a startling and unsettling insight, but not one unfamiliar to novelists and dramatists whose stock in trade is misfiring intentionality:

> Human thought is a terrible instrument! It is both our defence and our safeguard, the finest of all God's gifts. It is ours and it obeys us. We can project it into space, but once it is outside our feeble skull, it is too late and we are no longer in charge of it.[18]

De Musset's playful depiction of human thought as being somehow capable of extending creatively beyond the boundaries of ourselves reminds us of the dual approaches to religious life that we encountered at the beginning of chapter 1. There is the monastic *stabilitas* powerfully promoted by Benedict and Lugidus (among many others), and there is the outward, questing form of religious life exemplified in the knights of Chrétien of Troyes, in Dorothy, in the *gyrovagus*, in Spielberg's Roy Neary, and in the Stalker. Here, in the quote from de Musset, we find the same opposition between safety in locality, and danger in projection. While human thought remains inside our feeble skulls, it is obedient and ours; once outside the skull, however, it is its own boss, capricious even. To project our thoughts out into the world is to relinquish control over those thoughts. But if the world is itself composed of those projected thoughts, it follows that we have no control over the world either. Like Peter, we sink.

18. de Musset, *Confession of a Child*, 233.

The act of creation and loss of control are mutually entailed. Of course, Tarkovsky is steering a radically different course from Berkeley for whom the world is as stable and as regular as Lugidus or Benedict could wish on account of the wisdom and benevolence of its Author:

> [The ideas of sense] have a steadiness, order, and coherence, and are not excited at random ... but in a regular train or series, the admirable connexion whereof sufficiently testifies the wisdom and benevolence of its Author.[19]

In *Stalker*, on the other hand, there is no guarantee that the Zone will remain ordered and regular; we are repeatedly told that norms of space and time are disrupted, that the laws of nature do not hold here, and so neither—we must assume—does the lawgiver.

Removing Berkeley's guarantor God, Tarkovsky focusses on all that is left: our predicament and our faith. For Tarkovsky, Berkeley's God underpinning the rightness of our perceptions would have been too redolent of the stability he saw it as his duty to destroy. There is no stability aside from the false and self-serving stability of society; creation is inherently unstable, and the artist must reveal that truth. So, were we not after all correct to suggest that Tarkovsky's message is fundamentally iconoclastic and irreligious? Not at all. As I argued above, at the beginning of chapter 2, we need not accept the statements of Saints Benedict and Lugidus regarding the essential role of *stabilitas* as axiomatic for all religious life and witness. There is always the journey. Journeys are, by their very nature, risky, prone to the vicissitudes of changing circumstances, fraught with dangers and difficulties (rather like film shoots), and they may not always or apparently

19. Berkeley, *Treatise*, 113.

Faith

prove successful. Journeys that begin in triumph can end in humiliation, rejection, agony, and death.

Again, by removing a stabilizing God from the equation, Tarkovsky presents the possibility that the divine act of creation itself is a risky journey toward perfection, an act, therefore, of faith as foolhardy as the Stalker's. Seen in this light, God's creative act is less like an authoritative command, and more like a gift. According to Jean-Luc Marion, God gives "himself to be thought as love, hence as gift."[20] If Marion's radical postmodernism does not appeal or persuade, Catholic theologian David L. Schindler has also described creation as "a being-given . . . a participation in the self-diffusive generosity of God as good" and as "an act of love, which means that creatures come into being through an act of giving: to be a creature is to be a gift."[21] Bringing out the inescapable risk inherent in "self-diffusive generosity," John Macquarrie describes God's creative act in the following way:

> Being lets-be, but it does so only at risk to itself, only by giving itself and going out into openness.[22]

We are back with risk.

As an act of giving, creation is a risky ceding of control. So, Simone Weil is able to describe creation as abandonment and abdication;[23] "God could only create by hiding himself. Otherwise there would be nothing but himself."[24] Abandoning, hiding, all for the sake of giving; these are terms we could apply more or less precisely to the Zone.

20. Marion, *God without Being*, 49.
21. Schindler, "Given as Gift," 82, 81.
22. Macquarrie, *Principles of Christian Theology*, 217.
23. Weil, *Gateway to God*, 48, 54.
24. Weil, *Gravity and Grace*, 38.

And they can be summed up as sacrifice. As John Caputo recognizes, "the possibility of regret is a condition of the possibility of the gift."[25]

> The word by which God lets the world be must also be the word by which God lets the world go, letting Godself in for something that God did not bargain for or see coming.[26]

It is, in other words, an act of maximally generous weakness rather than an expression or function of power. All giving is giving up, self-sacrifice: "Give to everyone who begs from you; and if anyone takes away your goods, do not ask for them again."[27] The widow, "out of her poverty[,] has put in everything she had, all she had to live on."[28] In short, creation is cross-shaped. Vulnerability, risk-laden openness to suffering, is a consequence of loving generosity, and is therefore a consequence of creation.[29]

In the west, over thousands of years, we have grown used to the idea that the order, structure, and predictability of the universe are grounds for believing in an omnicompetent creator God who justly determines this orderly, structured and predictable universe precisely according to his purposes. In its most refined examples, this "cosmological" argument from apparent design to apparent (or disapparent) designer emphasizes the flawless and limitless intellect of God; creation is an expression (albeit a fallen and therefore marred one) of that flawless and limitless intellect. Berkeley's immaterialism is a relevant example.

---

25. Caputo, *Weakness of God*, 85.
26. Caputo, *Weakness of God*, 85.
27. Luke 6:30.
28. Mark 12:44.
29. See Moltmann, *Crucified God*, 237–38.

FAITH

What our reflection on *Stalker* has led us to ponder is the extent to which this model is still functional and helpful. In chapter 1, we encountered the "perhaps predicament," the brute fact of our fallibility. In chapter 2, we explored how our fallibility is bordered or structured into our lives, and then we looked at the historical-cultural idea of goalless yet subjectively transformative journey which stands in contrast to the *stabilitas* of the center. In chapter 3, we encountered the kingdom of God as an absurdity, insurgent and ubiquitous, that blows *stabilitas* wide open. And in chapter 4, we have focused on faith as folly. What set us off on this line of enquiry was our taking issue with Lugidus's claim that religion and stability are somehow mutually entailed. By comparing Jesus' parables of the kingdom with Shakespeare's "green world," and with the marginal Zone in *Stalker*, we characterized the kingdom of God as unlike any kingdom we have ever encountered. So much for the kingdom; what about the king? The king of such a kingdom would appear to be either weak or nonexistent, or mad. A kingdom, as we understand the term, implies *stabilitas*, and it is the king who guarantees or imposes that *stabilitas*. But this king's kingdom, as we explored it in chapter 3, is radically unstable and unpredictable and borderless. If we need to rethink what we mean by the kingdom of God, we perhaps also need to rethink what we mean by the Kingship of God. This king "through whom all things were made" is executed with criminals, a king mocked for being a "king," a king who chooses not to guard the kingdom, but to give it.

We began this section by thinking about faith. We found that faith, for Tarkovsky, was not a destination, a life choice, a ticket to ride, but the theological equivalent of gravity, the weakest of the fundamental forces which nonetheless is essential for the existence of everything and anything. In Gregory of Nyssa, we found that faith is our only epistemological resource. Faith impels the risk-laden outward movement, the creative act that is always manifested as gift, as sacrifice. From here it is a short (and well-trodden) step to the traditional Judeo-Christian mystic's argument, that in order for the world to come into existence, the Lion of the Tribe of Judah must become the slaughtered Lamb,[30] the "lamb slain before the foundation of the world."[31] God elects to be not-God, in a giving (sacrificing) of God's Word "through whom all things were made and through whom we exist."[32] But, in fact, Tarkovsky appears to be suggesting precisely the opposite in *Stalker*. Weakness—the weakness that is an expression of the freshness of being, the weakness of faith, the weakness of the fool—is the weakness of God. Weakness is therefore not a property God assumes, benignantly setting aside kingly power in order to create, but is itself a perfection, a fundamental characteristic of God's nature.

> God's foolishness is wiser than human wisdom, and God's weakness is stronger than human strength.[33]

The act of creation is not risky because it involves a divestment of power, but because that which is essentially weak—the poor widow, the victim, the Stalker—dares through faith to give everything, to assume the powerful position of donor. God has to forget that God is *not* God (sovereign, king, creator) in order to create. Here it is worth noting Derrida's point that giving entails "an absolute

---

30. Rev 5:5–6.
31. Rev 18:8.
32. 1 Cor 6:6.
33. 1 Cor 1:25.

forgetting, a forgetting that also absolves, that unbinds absolutely."[34] It is in the forgetting that the miracle occurs.

---

34. Derrida, *Given Time*, 16.

5

MIRACLE

Stalker falls apart in its final ten minutes. And it falls apart exquisitely.

Surprisingly little has been written about the final sequence of *Stalker*. This is surprising because it stands as one of the most arresting and arrestingly beautiful few minutes of action ever committed to film.

After a scene in the bar with the disappointed returnees from the Zone, shot as previously in black and white, the film switches again to color, as though we were back in the Zone. In a tightly framed tracking shot we follow the Stalker's disabled daughter in profile. And she appears to be walking! We hear the sound of her footsteps, we see her head moving along at walking pace in front of the landscape behind. Is this her "Peter on the water" moment?

It is only when the shot widens that the truth is revealed: the disabled girl is sitting on her father, the Stalker's shoulders; it is his footsteps we have been hearing. This is the sort of visual, cinematic trick that Tarkovsky normally eschews. The fact he has chosen to use a device of this sort at this point in the film suggests he is making an important point.

We had been expecting a miracle in the Room; we were denied. Now, we are led to feel we may be witnessing something marvelous, miraculous—only to be denied again. The second denial marks the nadir: nothing, precisely nothing, has occurred in the film to corroborate Professor Wallace's claims, or to justify the Stalker's faith. The starman's message of hope over the radio was a hoax; Ronnie Neary was right: "No, they're not for real." Defeated but clinging still to his faith, the Stalker rails against the Writer and the Professor for their faithlessness:

> Calling themselves intellectuals, those writers and scientists. They don't believe in anything! They've got the organ with which one believes atrophied for lack of use. They know they were "born for a purpose," "called upon!" Can people like that believe in anything?[1]

The most awful thing, according to the Stalker, is people's lack of need, their very strength in purpose and calling. They have mistaken needlessness for strength when they should have recognized the precise opposite: that their strength lies in their need—for faith.

In this moment, in this defeat, another border is imperceptibly crossed. It is a moment marked by Tarkovsky who, from this moment on in the film, quietly but categorically overturns all the conventions of his own film, destroying the *stabilitas*, demanding Bevans's "radical shift in perspective, a change of horizon—a conversion."[2] But the moment goes unmarked by the Stalker himself. Instead, he goes to bed.

1. Tarkovsky, *Stalker*.
2. Bevans, *Models of Contextual Theology*, 101.

Perfect in Weakness

Like a mother placating or indulging a child having a tantrum, the Wife offers to go with him to the Zone. But his despair is too deep: "No, you can't go there. What if it wouldn't work with you either?"[3] Rather than being an expression of doubt or faithlessness, I think this line touchingly articulates his faith: not the faith, as we have already said, of Abraham as described by Kierkegaard, but of Isaac, bound, betrayed, accepting. The Stalker's faith is not some towering, unshakeable achievement; it is fragile, vulnerable, flickering, but not extinguished. An angel may yet intercede. An unlikely saving hand may reach down through the rain, just at the moment we can hold on no longer.

And there we leave the Stalker: washed up, dust and ashes, finished, despairing of the world, but not of the Zone, not quite. Apart from the very opening shot of the bar, while the titles are still rolling, the character of the Stalker is in every single scene. Until the last ten minutes of the film. Prior to this final section, the question of our point of view has never been raised. This is the Stalker's story, and we remain with him throughout. We are never party to information or knowledge that is withheld from the Stalker. There is no authorial oversight, no Spielberg to take us from the Sonora desert in Mexico to Dharmsala in India, to Wyoming in pursuit of a starman, no Cervantes to keep us on the objective straight and narrow. He is our Stalker. And now he is gone.

Then, in the next shot, quite unexpectedly—and entirely breaking the film's own established principles—the Wife speaks to us directly, into the camera. From having been in an almost exclusively male environment, we are now being addressed by a female character. From male to female, from third person narrative to second person: the film appears to have been turned on its head; we find

3. Tarkovsky, *Stalker*.

MIRACLE

ourselves confronted by a newly confused and unstable set of conventions. Rather than impartial observers, we are now hearing this woman's moving confession. Lighting a cigarette, she assures us of her love for her husband:

> You had already learned, I expect, that he's God's fool. The whole neighbourhood was laughing at him. He was such a pitiful bungler . . . But he just came up to me and said, "Come with me." And off I went. And I've not regretted it once. Not once.[4]

In short, she went along with a joke. "Immediately, they left their nets and followed him."[5] To be awake, to be attentive to the call to "Come with me, follow me" is to dream, to imagine the impossible, faithfully, fearfully; to devise a reality, and to live within it, waiting for a punchline that may be forever withheld. Returning to Shakespeare and to St. Paul, we witness the Wife recognizing and responding to the wisdom of the fool. "God chose what is foolish in the world to shame the wise,"[6] to shame the Writer, the Professor, the border guards, the called, the purposeful. And this foolishness is transgressive, fanciful. So, Touchstone, the fool in *As You Like It*, says, "the truest poetry is our most feigning."[7] Truth and imagination are not at odds; on the contrary, they are, Touchstone suggests, intimately paired, necessary components of *epinoia* and of faith. This true yet feigning imagination is the organ which the Writer and the Professor have allowed to be atrophied. It is the organ that Theseus in *Midsummer Night's Dream* declares "bodies forth / the forms

---

4. Tarkovsky, *Andrei Tarkovsky: Collected Screenplays*, 415.
5. Matt 4:20.
6. 1 Cor 1:27.
7. Shakespeare, *As You Like It* 3.3.15.

103

of things unknown,"[8] that supersedes our rational faculty by apprehending "more than cool reason ever comprehends"[9] that "rises above all knowledge seized upon by [our own] ability as less than what [we] are in search of."[10] Tarkovsky's film is a "clearing away of conjectural reason,"[11] a *délire* declaration of faith in the possibility of prophetic imagination. It is only by being foolish, and faithful that we can dare to wrestle, like Jacob, with the "perhaps predicament" that lies as *Grenzsituation* at the ground of creation-as-gift; and as for Jacob so for us: the wound is our essence, it is who we are; it is a blessing.

In the long final shot of the film, we are back in color, and alone with Monkey, the disabled daughter of the Stalker and his Wife. She is seated at the head of a long, rough table on which are arranged three glasses, like an altar. We have been allowed into the presence of a mystery, ushered into the holy of holies. The shot opens through a veil of steam rising from a cup of tea, like incense. Monkey sits in profile, her hair covered by a gold scarf—a halo, lending the scene an iconic quality. Skakov recognizes the iconographic suggestion, but goes further, associating Monkey with the Virgin Mary.[12] The childishness and androgynous appearance of Monkey make this identification implausible to my mind. As the camera slowly pulls back, we hear Monkey's disembodied voice reciting a love poem. The poem, by Tiutchev, is not altogether appropriate for a child to read, and inappro-

---

8. Shakespeare, *Midsummer Night's Dream* 5.1.14–15.

9. Shakespeare, *Midsummer Night's Dream* 5.1.6.

10. "πᾶν τὸ καταλαμβανόμενον ὑπὸ τῆς ἰδίας δυνάμεως ὡς τοῦ ζητουμένου μικρότερον ὑπερβαίνων" (Gregory of Nyssa, *Contra Eunomium* 12 2 [*PG* 45:941A]).

11. "ἐκκαθήρας τὸν λογισμὸν τῶν τοιούτων ὑπονοιῶν" (Gregory of Nyssa, *Contra Eunomium* 12 2 [*PG* 45:941A]).

12. Skakov, *Cinema of Tarkovsky*, 162.

MIRACLE

priate also for a maidenly depiction of the Blessed Virgin, concerning as it does "the dull flame of desire" in a lover's lowered eyes. The poem—like so much in *Stalker*—is about eyes, about seeing. It opens with the lines:

> I love your eyes my dear,
> Their splendid, sparkling fire.[13]

As we have already noted, *Stalker* is about revelation, about seeing and being seen. The camera has focused throughout the film over and over again on the eyes of the characters. With her hard, inscrutable eyes, Monkey now stares at the glasses arranged on the table top. Then—slowly, falteringly at first—the glasses begin to move one by one across the surface of the table. Monkey moves the glasses with her mind, with her eyes. The eye, like the camera itself, is the means of the miracle, as well as its medium. For Tarkovksy, literally, seeing is believing, and—crucially—*vice versa*:

> "My teacher, let me see again." Jesus said to him,
> "Go; your faith has made you well."[14]

Seeing is an act of faith; watchers are believers. Perhaps in watching from Olympus, the Greek gods believed in us more than we ever believed in them.

As miracles go, Monkey's telekinetic conjuring trick is not much maybe. But it is enough. As the dandelion seeds that drift across the room break the frame of the shot, so the miracle breaks the frame of the movie. It changes everything.

Suppose for a moment Tarkovsky had elected to end the film with the Wife's declaration of her unconditional and self-sacrificial love for the Stalker. The film would stand as a stable psychological whole; we could

13. Tiutchev, quoted in Skakov, *Cinema of Tarkovsky*, 163.
14. Mark 10:51-52.

enjoy the irony that what the Stalker had been searching for throughout the film had, in a sense, been at home all along: the redemptive love of a good woman. Without losing its religious undertones, the film (were it to end with the Wife's speech) could be interpreted entirely (and movingly) psychologically and naturalistically. The futility of the men's quest would be ironically redeemed, according to this reading, by the speech of the Wife. It is her faith—in the strength and bonds of human love—that we are being asked to approve over and above the questing, male, romantic faith in the ultimately fruitless and supernatural. Tarkovsky himself has suggested that the Wife's speech is the culmination of *Stalker*:

> The arrival of the Stalker's wife in the café where they are resting confronts the Writer and the Scientist with a puzzling, to them incomprehensible, phenomenon. There before them is a woman who has been through untold miseries because of her husband, and has had a sick child by him; but she continues to love him with the same selfless, unthinking devotion as in her youth. Her love and her devotion are the final miracle which can be set against the unbelief, cynicism, moral vacuum poisoning the modern world, of which both the Writer and the Scientist are victims.[15]

This is an intriguing paragraph. By claiming the Wife's continuing love and devotion for her husband is the "final miracle," Tarkovsky seems to be wilfully disregarding Monkey's scene. His doing so only heightens the sense of mystery pervading that final, overtly (rather than metaphorically) miraculous image. Tarkovsky's evasion elevates the scene to ineffable status. More than ever, the

15. Tarkovsky, *Sculpting in Time*, 198.

MIRACLE

Monkey scene seems not to belong to the rest of the film. It becomes the fragment that does not belong to the whole, the fragment that is both disruption and distillation, both the puzzle and the key. Because in that final shot Tarkovsky presents us with something wildly at odds with an understanding of the film as a unified psychological whole; he gives us an out and out miracle (however insignificant), precisely something that breaks that unity apart. Tarkovsky's aim was clearly not stability. Quite the reverse. He disrupts the film—and disrupts every possible stable and easy interpretation of the film, even his own interpretation—by confronting us with this unassimilable challenge at the very end, a challenge that stands resolutely in defiance of any naturalistic or psychological reading of the film. The ending returns us with shocking force to the *serio ludere* with which we opened chapter 3, and the ludic distortions we discovered in the landscapes of Shakespeare's comedies and Brocéliande, and that were notably missing from La Mancha, and the Zone; Monkey's scene is like the punchline to a joke, but it is the punchline to the wrong joke, or a different joke. Rather than allowing the previously absurd elements of the joke suddenly to make sense, to come into readable focus, the final scene renders those elements doubly absurd. This joke comes apart at the seams, as it must, for jokes conform to syntactical structures and patterns within a language, while *délire* does not; all our interpretive strategies are undermined; our rationalistic and naturalistic guns are well and truly spiked.

Delivered in its dying moments, this scene is *Stalker*'s crux: Gregory's yawning divide that gapes within each and all of our interpretations of the phenomenal world and our place within it: the *Grenzsituation*, the divide between the natural and the supernatural, the mundane and the miracle; it is the epistemological "falling short" that gives rise to the "perhaps predicament" that demands the faith response; it lies behind the unstable, risky impulse outwards that impels all creative action; it is the desire of the limited for the limitless, the desire that wishes to push through the screen, smash through the mirror. In this sense, the miracle does not resolve the film as much as unresolve it; it is less of a closing than an opening. The journey ends not with a hoped-for destination, or in Act 5 when everyone returns from the forest to get married, or with Dorothy back at home, but like Moses continuing his climb toward—but never reaching—perfection.

In conclusion, I would like, briefly, to return to the Zone with the three journeyers. When the Stalker, the Writer, and the Professor stand on the threshold of the waterlogged Room, none of them dares enter. They look in impotently, weakly; their journey ends in disaster (the subject of all science-fiction, remember), and in failure. But by slowly tracking back, away from the men, untethering us from our generally close point of view, the camera draws attention to its own position. It dawns on us that we are in the Room. So who are we? The Stalker plainly describes those permitted to enter the Room: "Not the good, or the bad," he says, "but weak people."[16] We find the Room, our perfection, in weakness.

What, ultimately, is this Room we appear to have entered without noticing, almost by mistake, and from outside, *extra*? It is the chamber, the *camera*: that which is itself hidden, but which reveals, reveals us to ourselves. The Room, the camera, becomes a symbol of God's creative act. For to create is to reveal. God's revelation, like the camera's revelation, is an allowing of light into the darkness; exposure. Apocalypse.

16. Tarkovsky, *Stalker*.

Miracle

Earlier in the film, as the Stalker relates his redacted version of the Emmaus story, the camera pans back and forth across the sleeping-waking bodies of the Writer and the Professor. As it passes across the overcoat of the Professor, the camera reveals itself briefly—and presumably unintentionally—in the convex reflective surface of the Professor's shiny coat button. As Jesus reveals himself to the two disciples in the Emmaus story, so the camera reveals itself to us on the screen. It finally punctures the screen, opens the curtain, lifts the veil: on us as watched, and on that which watches us. Just for a moment, that span (from ultimate debasement to ultimate glory), that journey, is metaphorically present. We are beside God.[17]

---

17. Exod 33:20.

CODA

> Pay no attention to that man behind the curtain!
>
> —The Wizard, *The Wizard of Oz*

On the north wall of the apse of the sixth century basilica of St. Euphrasius in Poreč on the northern Adriatic coast of modern Croatia, there is an unprecedented mosaic depiction of the Visitation.[1] Unprecedented, because not only has the artist chosen to depict Mary and Elizabeth, but they have included an entirely non-scriptural character in the scene: a young woman or child, holding a curtain or veil aside in order to eavesdrop on the women's conversation. The girl's spying presence—like a camera—serves to underline the intimacy and humanity of the moment. But it also alerts us to the miracle, the cosmic, the impending incarnation. The portrayal of shock on the girl's face is naïve and touching; she holds a finger to her open mouth, as though she somehow recognizes that this apparently mun-

---

1. Luke 1:39–45.

Coda

dane meeting between two pregnant women is in fact the hinge on which the whole creation turns. The spying girl learns—as we must learn—to see, to have our eyes opened, to be watchers.

Like the servant girl in the mosaic, when Dorothy reaches the throne room of the kingdom of Oz, she also pulls aside a curtain, the screen, to reveal a king who is "a humbug," who declares himself to be neither great nor powerful, but who is "a very good man," able to reveal to the heartless Tinman, the cowardly Lion, and the brainless Scarecrow that what they had needed, what they had been looking for, they already had; who transforms them by being a camera, by showing them themselves. A king who gives.

> Tinman: How can I ever thank you enough?
>
> Wizard: Well, you can't![2]

And the sixth-century mosaic stands also, I suggest, as a perfect model for cinema itself: the curtain the girl holds aside is the screen by means of which we are vouchsafed a privileged, snatched glimpse of a world. Mary and Elizabeth, like the Wizard, are at once shielded and revealed by the screen, as are we.

So, in the mosaic, we have a camera (the girl) who sees for us, and a screen (the curtain) on and through which we gaze, but there remains one element missing. Above the arch of the basilica's apse is an image of Christ holding open a book in which are written the words *ego sum vera lux*. Here is the projector, the source of light. Apocalypse is not a lifting of the veil, but the bringing to it—and to us—of transformative light and life.

---

2. Fleming, *Wizard of Oz*.

BIBLIOGRAPHY

Auerbach, Erich. *Mimesis: The Representation of Reality in Western Literature*. Translated by Willard R. Trask. Princeton: Princeton University Press, 1968.

Austen, Jane. *Northanger Abbey, Lady Susan, The Watsons, and Sanditon*. The World's Classics. Oxford: Oxford University Press, 1980.

Ballard, J. G. *A User's Guide to the Millennium: Essays and Reviews*. London: HarperCollins, 1996.

Balthasar, Hans Urs von. *Presence and Thought: An Essay on the Religious Philosophy of Gregory of Nyssa*. Translated by Mark Sebanc. San Francisco: Ignatius, 1995.

Barker, Howard. "49 Asides for Tragic Theatre." In *The Routledge Drama Anthology and Sourcebook: From Modernism to Contemporary Performance*, edited by Maggie B. Gale and John F. Deeney, 653–55. London: Routledge, 2010.

Baxter, Richard. *The Poetical Fragments of Richard Baxter*. 4th ed. London: Pickering, 1821.

Bergman, Ingmar. *The Magic Lantern: An Autobiography*. Translated by Joan Tate. New York: Viking, 1988.

Berkeley, George. *Three Dialogues between Hylas and Philonous*. Oxford Philosophical Texts. Oxford: Oxford University Press, 1998.

———. *A Treatise Concerning the Principles of Human Knowledge*. Oxford Philosophical Texts. Oxford: Oxford University Press, 1998.

Bibliography

Bevans, Stephen B. *Models of Contextual Theology*. New York: Orbis, 2002.

Bird, Robert. *Andrei Tarkovsky: Elements of Cinema*. London: Reaktion, 2008.

Bolaño, Roberto. *The Unknown University*. Translated by Laura Healy. London: Macmillan, 2015.

Brueggemann, Walter. *The Prophetic Imagination*. 2nd ed. Minneapolis: Fortress, 2001.

Burkert, Walter. *Creation of the Sacred: Tracks of Biology in Early Religions*. Gifford Lectures, 1988–1989. Cambridge, MA: Harvard University Press, 1996.

Caputo, John D. *The Weakness of God: A Theology of the Event*. Bloomington: Indiana University Press, 2006.

Cavell, Stanley. *The World Viewed: Reflections on the Ontology of Film*. Enlarged ed. Harvard Film Studies. Cambridge, MA: Harvard University Press, 1979.

Cervantes. *Don Quixote*. Translated by J. M. Cohen. Harmondsworth: Penguin, 1950.

Chrétien de Troyes. *Arthurian Romances*. Translated by William W. Kibler. London: Penguin, 1991.

Collicutt, Johanna. *The Psychology of Christian Character Formation*. London: SCM, 2015.

Deleuze, Gilles. *Cinema II: The Time-Image*. Translated by Hugh Tomlinson and Robert Galeta. London: Bloomsbury, 2013.

de Musset, Alfred. *The Confession of a Child of the Century*. Translated by David Coward. London: Penguin, 2012.

Derrida, Jacques. *Given Time: I. Counterfeit Money*. Translated by Peggy Kamuf. Chicago: University of Chicago Press, 1992.

Dodds, E. R. *Proclus: The Elements of Theology*. Oxford: Clarendon, 1933.

———., ed. *Journals and Letters of Stephen Mackenna*. London: Constable, 1936.

Dorsky, Nathaniel. "Devotional Cinema." In *The Religion and Film Reader*, edited by Jolyon Mitchell and S. Brent Plate, 407–15. New York: Routledge, 2007.

Dyer, Geoff. *Zona: A Book about a Film about a Journey to a Room*. Edinburgh: Cannongate, 2012.

Fiennes, Sophie, dir. *The Pervert's Guide to the Cinema*. 2006; Written and presented by Slavoj Žižek. London: Mischief Films. DVD.

Fleming, Victor, dir. *The Wizard of Oz*. 1939; Los Angeles: Metro-Goldwyn-Mayer. Burbank, CA: Warner Home Video, 2014. DVD.

Bibliography

Francis of Assisi and Clare of Assisi. *Francis and Clare: The Complete Works*. Translated by Regis J. Armstrong and Ignatius C. Brady. New York: Paulist, 1982.

Frye, Northrop. *The Anatomy of Criticism: Four Essays*. London: Penguin, 1990.

Glazer, Jonathan, dir. *Under the Skin*. 2013; London: Studiocanal, 2014. DVD.

Gregory of Nyssa. *The Life of Moses*. Translated by Abraham Malherbe and Everett Ferguson. New York: Paulist, 1978.

Hammarskjöld, Dag. *Markings*. Translated by Leif Sjöberg and W. H. Auden. New York: Vintage Spiritual Classics, 2006.

Harper, Ralph. *On Presence: Variations and Reflections*. Baltimore: Johns Hopkins University Press, 2006.

Heidegger, Martin. *Parmenides*. Translated by André Schuwer and Richard Rojcewicz. Bloomington: Indiana University Press, 1998.

Hynek, J. Allen. *The UFO Experience: A Scientific Inquiry*. London: Corgi, 1974.

Jantzen, Grace M. "Touching (in) the Desert: Who Goes There?" In *Derrida and Religion: Other Testaments*, edited by Yvonne Sherwood and Kevin Hart, 375–92. New York: Routledge, 2005.

Jewett, Robert. "St. Paul at the Movies: The Apostle's Dialogue with American Culture." In *The Religion and Film Reader*, edited by Jolyon Mitchell and S. Brent Plate, 358–60. New York: Routledge, 2007.

Johnston, Robert K. "Reel Spirituality: Theology and Film in Dialogue." In *The Religion and Film Reader*, edited by Jolyon Mitchell and S. Brent Plate, 312–22. New York: Routledge, 2007.

Kierkegaard, Søren. *Fear and Trembling*. Translated by Alastair Hannay. London: Penguin, 1985.

Kreitzer, Larry J. "The New Testament in Fiction and Film: On Reversing the Hermeneutical Flow." In *The Religion and Film Reader*, edited by Jolyon Mitchell and S. Brent Plate, 370–73. New York: Routledge, 2007.

Lane, Belden C. *The Solace of Fierce Landscapes: Exploring Desert and Mountain Spirituality*. Oxford: Oxford University Press, 1998.

Latzel, Edwin. "The Concept of Ultimate Situation in Jaspers' Philosophy." In *The Philosophy of Karl Jaspers*, edited by Paul Arthur Schlipp. New York: Tudor, 1957.

Lecercle, Jean-Jacques. *Philosophy through the Looking-Glass: Language, Nonsense, Desire*. London: Hutchinson, 1985.

Bibliography

L'Engle, Madeleine. *Walking on Water: Reflections on Faith and Art*. New York: Convergent, 2016.

Levao, Ronald. *Renaissance Minds and their Fictions: Cusanus, Sidney, Shakespeare*. Berkeley: University of California Press, 1985.

MacIntyre, Alasdair. *God, Philosophy, Universities: A Selective History of the Catholic Philosophical Tradition*. Lanham: Rowman & Littlefield, 2009.

Macquarrie, John. *Principles of Christian Theology*. Rev. ed. London: SCM, 1977.

Marion, Jean-Luc. *Being Given: Toward a Phenomenology of Givenness*. Translated by Jeffrey L. Kosky. Stanford: Stanford University Press, 2002.

———. *God Without Being*. Translated by Thomas A. Carlson. Chicago: Chicago University Press, 1991.

Martin, Joel W., and Conrad E. Ostwalt. *Screening the Sacred: Religion, Myth, and Ideology in Popular American Film*. Boulder: Westview, 1995.

Mitchell, Jolyon. "Understanding Religion and Film in 'Postsecular' Russia." In *Religion in Contemporary European Cinema: The Postsecular Constellation*. Edited by Costica Bradatan and Camil Ungureanu. New York: Routledge, 2014.

Mitchell, Jolyon, and S. Brent Plate. *The Religion and Film Reader*. New York: Routledge, 2012.

Moltmann, Jürgen. *The Crucified God*. Translated by R. A. Wilson and John Bowden. London: SCM, 2001.

Nolan, Steve. "Towards a New Religious Film Criticism: Using Film to Understand Religious Identity Rather than Locate Cinematic Analogue." In *Mediating Religion: Conversations in Media, Religion and Culture*, edited by Jolyon Mitchell and Sophia Marriage, 169–78. London: T. & T. Clark, 2006.

O'Brien, Fran. *The Third Policeman*. London: HarperCollins, 2007.

Parrish, Robert, dir. *Journey to the Far Side of the Sun* (*Doppelgänger* in the UK), 1969; London: Universal Pictures, 2008. DVD.

Schindler, David L. "The Given as Gift: Creation and Disciplinary Abstraction in Science." *Communio* 38 (Spring 2011) 52–102.

Skakov, Nariman. *The Cinema of Tarkovsky: Labyrinths of Space and Time*. London: Tauris, 2012.

Sölle, Dorothy. *The Window of Vulnerability*. Minneapolis: Fortress, 1990.

Sontag, Susan. "The Imagination of Disaster." In *Against Interpretation and Other Essays*, 209–25. London: Penguin, 2009.

Bibliography

Southern, Richard. *The Making of the Middle Ages*. London: Pimlico, 1993.

Spielberg, Steven, dir. *Close Encounters of the Third Kind*. 1977; Culver City, CA: Columbia Pictures Industries, 2011. DVD.

Talbot Rice, David. *Byzantine Art*. London: Pelican, 1954.

Tarkovsky, Andrei. *Andrei Tarkovsky: Collected Screenplays*. Translated by William Powell and Natasha Synessios. London: Faber, 1999.

———. *Andrei Tarkovsky: Interviews*, edited by John Gianvito. Jackson: University Press of Mississippi, 2006.

———. *Sculpting in Time: Reflections on the Cinema*. Translated by Kitty Hunter-Blair. Austin: University of Texas Press, 1986.

———. *Time within Time: The Diaries 1970–1986*. Translated by Kitty Hunter-Blair. London: Faber, 1994.

Tarkovsky, Andrei, dir. *Stalker*. 1979; Moscow: Mosfilm. London: Artificial Eye, 2002. DVD.

Tillich, Paul. *Dynamics of Faith*. New York: Harper, 1958.

Tracy, David. "Fragments: The Spiritual Situation of our Times." In *God, the Gift and Postmodernism*, edited by John D. Caputo and Michael J. Scanlon, 170–81. Bloomington: Indiana University Press, 1999.

Waddell, Helen. *The Wandering Scholars*. 7th ed. London: Constable, 1934.

Weil, Simone. *Gateway to God*. Translated and edited by David Raper. London: Collins, 1974.

———. *Gravity and Grace*. Translated by Emma Crawford and Mario von der Ruhr. London: Routledge, 2002.

Wisdom, John. *Philosophy and Psycho-analysis*. Berkeley: University of California Press, 1964.

Wittgenstein, Ludwig. *Culture and Value*. Translated by Peter Winch. Chicago: University of Chicago Press, 1984.

Wolff, Philippe. *The Awakening of Europe*. Harmondsworth: Penguin, 1968.

Lightning Source UK Ltd.
Milton Keynes UK
UKHW041238200622
404686UK00004B/1184